Praise For

D1685606

THE UKCAT STUDY GUIDE

"The strategy laid out in this guide helped me achieve a score in the 9th decile having only achieved one in the 4th decile last year"

- Danny, scored 2940

"The study guide gave a really good basis and 'plan for action' for my UKCAT revision and massively helped me achieve a score I couldn't have dreamt of when I first started practising!"

- Sarah, scored 2870

"People who are beginners and want to jump straight to constructive studying, this book is highly recommended. The schedule and recommended book list it provided will save you time groping around in the dark"

- Han-Ting, scored 2740

"All you need is this guide and some practice questions"

- Dana, scored 2850

"A good guide with respect to assessing which areas you need to work on the most. Helps you create a structured study plan which otherwise I would not have done"

- Jack, scored 2830

"Great platform to help further your understanding of the Aptitude test. Helps improve strategy and focus your practise to allow for the best possible outcome"

- Hafsah, scored 2720

"This was helpful in understanding the UKCAT strategically and helped me improve my score a lot"

- Monica, scored 2540

"This study guide is definitely different from other UKCAT resources. It is very specific in guiding you on how you should improve based on your individual weaknesses. Practising UKCAT questions alongside this guide really helps to narrow down which sections I should focus on"

- Tiana, scored 2870

"For those who do not know where to begin with UKCAT revision, like me, this guide is absolutely perfect"

- Ishan, scored 2900

"Would've been lost without it! Really helped structure my preparation"

- Gabriella, scored 2560

"The study guide helped me immensely with preparation techniques and helped me gain more confidence in my abilities as the test approached"

- Natacha, scored 2850

"I really liked it and found all the advice really helpful, especially for the abstract reasoning section. I also liked how it helped me organise my revision and prioritise what to spend the most time on."

- Bethanh, scored 3200

"This guide helped me to effectively identify my weakest section of the UKCAT and improve upon it. I think this had the biggest positive impact on my total score because it meant that I was no longer aimlessly doing questions but instead targeted focused revision"

- Serena, scored 2710

"This guide completely changed how I approached the UKCAT"

- Mason, scored 2820

THE UKCAT STUDY GUIDE

How to Score in the Top Percentile

The tactics, tips and strategies I used to achieve a UKCAT score in the 90th Percentile

Michael O. Carter

www.theukcatblog.com

Printed in the United Kingdom

First Printing, 2018

ISBN 978-1-9999390-0-7 (paperback version)

ISBN 978-1-9999390-1-4 (eBook version)

Published by THE UKCAT BLOG LIMITED

www.theukcatblog.com

To all the subscribers and followers of THE UKCAT BLOG, old and new, thank you for the gift of your support. I only hope this UKCAT study guide can begin to repay you for all the feedback and support that you've given me.

Here's to you and your continued success

Contents

My Story and Why You Need This Book

'King's College, University of London – unsuccessful'. There it was. My UCAS homepage was relentless in its confirmation that, as of February 2010, I received rejections from all four medical schools I applied to. I sat at the desk in my bedroom in a weird semi-conscious state thinking it was the end of the world. Later, I wandered online trying to consider alternative options, I remember I was so utterly dispirited that I was unable to bring myself to share the news with my family.

So, what now? I had applied the previous October with confidence that I would get at least one offer. I had straight "A" predictions for my A-levels (Chemistry, Physics and Maths) and amazing work experience at my local hospital to support my application.

I had accumulated 5 month's work experience as a volunteer in the Diabetes Clinic at Darrent Valley Hospital in Dartford, I was well briefed on NHS current affairs and had been given so much valuable guidance from healthcare professions and medical students.

Yet, I had failed to convert all the support into a single offer! I despaired at the thought of going through the long application process again. But worst of all was the fear gnawing away at me: that I would never be a doctor!

"Making your mark on the world is hard. If it were easy, everybody would do it. But it's not. It takes patience, it takes commitment, and it comes with plenty of failures along the way. The real test is not whether you avoid this failure because you won't. It's whether you let it harden or shame you into inaction, or whether you learn from it; whether you choose to persevere" - **Barack Obama, US President from 2009 – 2017**

After a few days of pathetic wallowing, I decided to put it behind me. I came across the quote by Barack Obama and decided, that moment, to preserve! My ambition did not change, final A-level exams were fast approaching so I had to refocus quickly if I was going to give myself a fighting chance of reapplying. At least the shock of rejection had not depleted my motivation to work; I was desperate to prove the universities wrong by achieving my predicted grades.

It took a lot of hard work and determination, but I did it! I achieved 3 A's in Physics, Chemistry and Maths, and decided I was going to take a gap year and reapply.

Once my A-levels were out of the way, I felt free to explore why I had failed to secure a place. All my medical school choices rejected me at application review due to my below the par score in the United Kingdom Clinical Aptitude Test (UKCAT). I discovered that the year I first applied there were over 80,000 applications for medicine, that was one place for every 10 applicants! To fall at just one hurdle meant immediate rejection. I soon realised that I was so naive to have been so confident of an offer. While my application was strong in some parts I had let myself down with my UKCAT score. I was so determined to beat the odds so I practised harder for the exam the second time.

Before my second attempt at the UKCAT, I signed up for a two-day crash course in London and spent an additional six weeks practising questions. The fate-deciding two hours in front of a computer screen eventually came around and surprisingly it was not as terrifying as the previous year. I did score a higher average of 640 but I was a little bit disappointed; it was not as high as I was hoping. However, I still applied, hoping my A-level grades and proven commitment would tilt things in my favour, but unfortunately it did not. I was still rejected by all my choices! To be fair, I had been invited to two interviews but still was not able to convert them into an offer, so what now? In all honesty, I gave up. I decided to take on my 5th choice and study Pharmacology at the University of Manchester instead.

Pharmacology was amazing, learning about different medications, their sources, chemical properties, biological effects and therapeutic uses. I particularly enjoyed exploring drug interactions in biological systems and how chemical formulation interacts with living tissue. In third year there was a lot of focus on clinical trials, understanding how animals were used in research and the critical role they play in the scientific understanding of biomedical systems leading to successful drugs, therapies and cures for diseases like Hypertension, Diabetes, Cataracts, Obesity, Seizures, Respiratory problems, Deafness, Parkinson's disease, Alzheimer's disease, Cancer, Cystic fibrosis, HIV, Heart disease, Muscular dystrophy and Spinal cord injuries.

However, I soon realised that a career in Pharmacology might not be for me. I remember the moment like it was yesterday, it was at the Stopford building, the main lecture building for life science related courses, when I had to inject a live rat with saline solution during an animal handling exercise (do not worry, saline is a harmless mixture of salt and water which is used to train students on proper animal handling techniques).

"Are you nervous?" my supervisor asked as I was stalling.

"I'm good. Just trying to figure out the logistics" I replied.

That was not entirely true. It was hard to stay cool given the circumstance, I was trying to adopt the handling technique taught to reduce animal stress and decrease the likelihood of getting bitten. Rodents were popular research subjects because their genetic, biological and behaviour characteristics closely resemble those of humans, and many symptoms of human conditions can be replicated in rodents. Most of the mice and rats used in our clinical practice were inbred so that, other than sex differences, they are almost identical genetically. This helps make the results of the trials more uniform; according to the National Human Genome Research Institute as a minimum requirement, mice used in experiments must be of the same purebred species. Many Manchester students might not be aware that on the top floor of this Stopford building is a huge 'secret' research facility with high level security. Before you can even access this floor as a student you are required to pass some nationally recognised test and fill in a non-disclosure agreement (NDA). This was where all our clinical practices were being carried out and it gave me first hand exposure to life as a clinical research scientist (my back-up career choice since medicine wasn't working out). Nonetheless, I took a deep breath, grabbed the rodent, it squirmed a bit - I dropped it!

"Do you need a hand, mate?" my supervisor asked impatiently

"I'm good, was just caught by surprise, going to give it another try" I replied.

At that very moment, all of a sudden, I became self-aware, I began to notice the queue of students behind me waiting their turn with cringing looks coupled with excitement, kind of the look trainee doctors have when witnessing a baby being delivered during medical training. I also realised it had been 10 whole minutes and I was no closer to successfully handling the rodent and injecting it with saline.

'5 minutes to go before it's the end of your turn" the supervisor reminded.

It was now or never, I said to myself. I took another deep breath and went for it. After two more tries and about thirty seconds to spare, I successfully handled the rat, holding it with my left hand and injecting the solution with my right without a single bite, I remember a few mates bragging they did it in one go but I was just glad I passed. I heard a rumour that a girl on the course got bitten and fainted. She dropped the rat and they had to lock down the entire practice area to prevent the rodent from escaping; not sure how true that story is but it gave me the confidence I needed to know that things could have gone a lot worse.

"Every failure brings with it a seed of an equivalent lesson" - Napoleon Hill

Overall, I did enjoy clinical practice but with time, I realised it was not what I want to do for the rest of my life - it's hard to put into words why I felt this way, and over the years I have never really figured it out - all I can say is that it doesn't give me that 'feel good' feeling I normally get when I'm passionate about something. For me, the theoretical side of Pharmacology was more appealing. There was a lot of crossover with the medicine curriculum, so I had to take a few lectures in the medical building. This gradually rekindled my passion to become a doctor and in the summer before my final year I decided to apply to graduate-entry medicine.

This would be my third time applying! I was determined not to fail again, I took the time to reflect on my previous attempts at the exam and work out where I could improve. Upon reflection, I came up with a preparation plan that would accomplish **FOUR** things:

- Effectively identify weak areas in the UKCAT and improve my reasoning skills in a short amount of time.

- Learn exam strategies and techniques to improve performance in each section.

- Effectively practice questions to increase familiarity with the exam as well as potential traps laid out by examiners.

- Include a feedback loop and performance indicators to regularly assess progress over time and adapt preparation accordingly.

After seven weeks of studying and adopting this new strategy, the UKCAT finally came around and this time I could feel my hands sweating. I eventually managed to keep my cool and kept going over the 'study notes' I had put together from my revision.

"Michael O. Carter" the test supervisor yells with a strong Mancunian accent across the test centre waiting room.

"Yes?" I nervously replied

"Computer number 16 is now available for you to take your test", she continued.

I got up and walked towards the screen. All I could think of at that moment, as I was walking over, was that my dream to become a doctor came down to this test. I had three A's at A level under my belt and was on track to get at least a 2.1 in Pharmacology - I strongly believed a good UKCAT score would tilt things in my favour.

I sat down, logged in and the test began.

Arguably the longest two hours of my life but eventually, it was over. I walked out and waited for my results in the waiting room.

A few minutes later, "Michael O. Carter!" supervisor yelled again.

"Here is your score report. Good work!" she praised before handing me a piece of paper.

I stared down at it, I couldn't believe my eyes, I did it! I exceeded my target score with an average of 710 in each section (Total of 2840), my entire approach to preparing for the exam paid off. I went from an average of 600 to 710 by strategically adapting my preparation.

Over the ensuing weeks I began getting a lot of questions from family friends planning to apply to Medicine and Dentistry the following year; my mum had pretty much told her friends I was going to be a doctor (when in fact I had not even applied at this point).

I was so busy balancing my studies, part-time job and volunteer experience that I thought it would be easier to create a blog that would address all their questions instead of replying individually. The general idea of the blog was to share the tips and techniques that worked for me when I took the test. After a few months, to my surprise, the blog started getting a bit of traffic, I remember it reaching 1,000 monthly visits after 5 months. I couldn't believe it! The result inspired me to include more advice and tips for preparing for the exam. Today, the blog is visited by an average of 10,000 students each month and the numbers continue to rise. The testimonials and feedback continue to inspire me to continue updating the website and this guide.

A year after launch, I would occasionally get emails from readers seeking more specific advice on how to prepare for the exam. Some of the most common questions included;

- Where do I start with my UKCAT revision?
- What amount of preparation time should I give each section?
- What is the minimum UKCAT score I need to achieve?
- Is 1 month enough time to prepare for the exam?
- How do you save time with the onscreen calculator?
- How did you attempt practice questions?
- How many mocks would you recommend doing before the test?
- Can I improve my verbal reasoning skills in 1 month?
- How did you keep motivated with your UKCAT preparation?

Little did I know where questions like this would take me. It was these types of questions that birthed this study guide.

"An expert is a person who has made all the mistakes that can be made in a narrow field"

- Niels Bohr, Physicist & Nobel Prize Winner

The main mistake I made the first two times I prepared for the test was that I practiced loads of questions but had no clear strategy, besides learning from the answers - I thought I was improving but in actual fact I was only familiarising myself with the questions in the exam. In hindsight, it is no surprise my score didn't improve much the second time. I was, essentially, just getting used to the type of questions in the exam - this is what I believe is the most common mistake made by most candidates when preparing for the UKCAT.

There is a long list of books and courses that focus on practice questions rather than preparation or exam strategies. I would argue that strategy, for overall preparation and attempting the individual subtests, is far more important because the UKCAT doesn't contain any curriculum content, rather your cognitive and reasoning abilities are being tested. Therefore, it is more effective to place emphasis on strategies for each subtest rather than 'improving familiarity' with the test. The third time I took the exam, I incorporated just that, and with an effective feedback loop I not only familiarized myself with the exam but also significantly improved my reasoning skills; thus, my overall score.

This book covers both the preparation strategy I used and over 200 exam strategies, tips and tactics for each subtest, I encourage you find the ones that work for you and master them before your big day.

Here is the step-by-step process you will follow to achieve UKCAT success:

❶ **Set** introduces concepts for setting a target score by understanding how universities use the UKCAT. For example, what is the minimum score needed to be invited for an interview? This section explores all the key factors to determine a target practice score.

❷ **Identify** explains an effective step-by-step approach for discovering weak areas in the exam and shortcomings in reasoning skills.

❸ **Prioritise** introduces a new approach for determining the order of dealing with the UKCAT subtests. Which subtest to spend the most time preparing for, and by how much.

❹ **Improve** recommends over 200 proven exam techniques, tips and strategies to boost performance in each section. From pattern finding strategies in the abstract reasoning section to comprehension and time saving techniques in the verbal section.

❺ **Practice** introduces sub-strategies for attempting practice questions and boosting productively. Learn techniques for boosting productivity and studying efficacy. Also includes advice on picking resources such as practice books, online courses, crash courses and tuitions.

❻ **Assess** introduces key performance indicators (KPIs) to evaluate progress over time. Prepare more effectively by keeping an eye on the indicators introduced in this section.

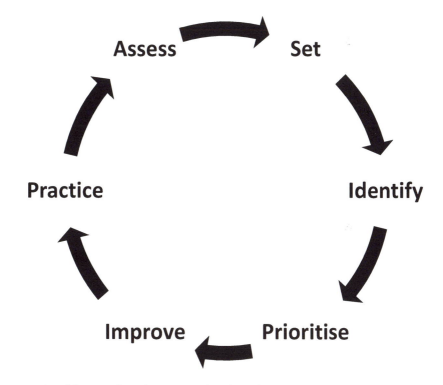

I should note that this entire book is designed to be very specific in guiding you on how to improve based on your individual weaknesses and jumpstart you into constructive studying.

Last but not the least, I've included a **Companion Course** that includes free access to the following, they are as follows:

- **Private Facebook Study Group** provides the opportunity to learn and get new perspectives from other students taking the UKCAT in the same year. Share advice and learn from one another as you prepare for the exam.

- **30-day Study Plan** manages your time by applying the key concepts in this book. Includes weekly goals to be completed over 30 days and weekly reminders to ensure you are on track.

I'm about to show you step-by-step how to achieve a UKCAT score in the 90th percentile. I remember looking on The Student Room (TSR) a while ago and reading posts from successful applicants claiming that they did not really prepare for the UKCAT, they only familiarised themselves with the questions. Further stating that preparation will not significantly improve an applicant's score! I am living proof that those claims are utter rubbish! It is **POSSIBLE** to significantly increase your UKCAT score and I'm going to show you how I did it.

Some exercises in this book may require you to write things down. To help you, you can download the worksheets and templates mentioned and utilised throughout the book from the Companion Course. I've also included surprise bonus exercises to help keep you motivated.

It is truly an honour sharing this strategy with you, it was a huge game changer for me and I hope it does the same for you. Take a deep breath and let me guide you on your journey to UKCAT success.

I am and will continue to be a humble tutor to you all.

Mike

What You Will Need

Here is a list of the materials you will need before you begin the UKCAT study guide. I recommend getting them in place before you begin step 1 of the strategy.

❶ **A notepad**: Any notepad will do, but I recommend an A7 mini notepad to encourage you make shorter and more effective study notes.

❷ **Official UKCAT website:** The official exam website has helpful resources and practice questions to help prepare for the exam. This is where we will begin our preparation!

❸ **A UKCAT Practice book:** There are many UKCAT books with thousands of practice questions. Every year I shortlist the best ones and share them on the blog. Check out my recommended UKCAT practice books for the year at www.theukcatblog.com. I do not recommend buying all of them instead pick the most suitable.

❹ **An online UKCAT Course:** The UKCAT is a computer-based exam so it is essential to invest in an online course that mimics the testing environment to put the tips, techniques and strategies in this guide to practice. The best courses offer additional tutorials and mock tests, so make sure to pick the most suitable. Check out my recommended online UKCAT courses for the year on the blog too.

❺ **30-day Study Plan:** The 30-day study plan is designed to structure your preparation and add urgency by giving you small goals over 30 days, it incorporates the core principles of the guide. Get your 30-day plan when you sign up to the free companion course.

❻ **Companion Course:** The companion course includes exercises, additional tips and exam advice from myself and other successful candidates.

I must stress that it is not mandatory to invest in a practice book or online course, but it will give you a massive advantage over other candidates as you will gain more familiarity with the spectrum of question-types and conditions of the exam. A survey by the exam board showed that use of these third-party materials correlated with higher scores in the exam.

Study Guide Companion Course

To help take your preparation to the next level, I created a free Companion Course that you can get access to which includes a downloadable 30-day study plan, bonus tips, access to private study group and links to the resources mentioned in this book. This is your first step toward success with the content in this book, so I highly recommend you sign up now. I'll be adding more material in the companion course over time, so make sure to visit the web address below and get free instant access to it now! See you on the inside!

Visit the following link to get access to your UKCAT Study Guide Companion Course:

WWW.THEUKCATBLOG.COM/UKCAT-COMPANION-COURSE

Step 1: Set

Setting Your Target Practice Score

A few years ago, I received an email from someone named Jade, a medicine applicant and regular reader of the blog. I get a lot of emails from readers but this one had an eye-catching subject line.

Subject: I got 690 is that good enough?

Hi Michael, I did my UKCAT yesterday and got 2760 as an overall score (VR -590, QR -760, DM -680, AR-730 and Band 2). I've been following your blog and the advice has been great so far and was really helpful in preparing for my UKCAT. Can you please advise if 2760 is a good enough score to apply to Medicine? Kind Regards

- Jade

I regularly get similar questions like this from readers and I usually find myself replying by asking the same question every time:

Hi Jade, Thank you for the email. Glad you found the blog helpful. With regards to your question, how does your first choice assess the UKCAT? Regards,

- Mike

The most common response from readers is that they have no clue, whilst some are not sure. In Jade's case, she mentioned her choice stated on their website they did not have a minimum UKCAT requirement and rank applicants based on their overall application where the UKCAT is taken into account.

Universities use the UKCAT differently, some have a cut-off where a score good enough for admittance into one university might not be good enough for another. Whilst others rely more on a ranking approach where the UKCAT is one of many components taken into consideration to rank applicants.

Nonetheless, it is of great importance to understand how your choice assesses the UKCAT because it helps understand if your score is good enough, even though, in some cases your choice may not have a minimum requirement. All universities part of the UKCAT consortium assess the UKCAT in some way; it is by understanding this 'assessment' you can set a target practice score, i.e. a goal during your UKCAT preparation. To help further explain this, let's take a quick look at the UKCAT and its format.

UKCAT Format

The UKCAT is a computer-administered exam lasting 2 hours. The test consists of five parts: Verbal Reasoning, Quantitative Reasoning, Abstract Reasoning, Decision Making and Situational Judgement.

UKCAT Subtests			
Subtest	*Time Allowed*	*Number of Questions*	*Time Per Question*
Verbal Reasoning	21 minutes	44	30 seconds
Quantitative Reasoning	24 minutes	36	38 seconds
Abstract Reasoning	13 minutes	55	15 seconds
Decision Making	31 minutes	29	64 seconds
Situational Judgement	26 minutes	69	22 seconds

Each of the five parts of the UKCAT is in a multiple-choice format and is timed separately, they are as follows:

Verbal reasoning subtest: According to the official UKCAT site "the verbal section tests the ability to read and think carefully". You are given 21 minutes to complete 44 questions. Some questions assess critical reasoning skills, where you are required to make inferences and draw conclusions. Others might be an incomplete statement or a question, with four response options where you are required to pick the best or most suitable answer from the options provided. For other questions, your task is to read each passage carefully and then decide whether the statement provided is True, False or Can't Tell.

Quantitative Reasoning: According to the official UKCAT site "tests the ability to solve numerical problems". You are given 24 minutes to complete 36 questions. The problems are at the GCSE level and includes tables, charts and graphs, where you are required to extract relevant information. A simple on-screen calculator is made available to use in this section

Abstract Reasoning: According to the official site "the abstract reasoning tests the ability to spot patterns amongst abstract shapes where distracting patterns may lead to incorrect conclusions". The test measures the ability to critically evaluate, generate hypotheses and change track if necessary. You are given 13 minutes to complete 55 questions. The subtest includes 4 different types of questions which we will cover in more detail later in the book.

Decision Making: According to the official site "tests the ability to apply logic to reach a decision or conclusion, evaluate arguments and analyse statistical information". This is a relatively new subtest where some questions will have 4 answer options with one correct answer, others may give you a statement options where you are required to place a 'yes' or 'no' next to each statement. You are given 31 minutes to complete 29 questions and will be provided with an onscreen calculator for the subtest.

Situational Judgement: According to the official site "tests your capacity to understand real world situations and identify critical factors and appropriate behaviour in dealing with them". You will be given 26 minutes to complete 69 questions, there are two types of questions in this subtest, we will cover them in detail later in the book.

For further information about the exam and individual sections, see the official UKCAT Website on:

WWW.UKCAT.AC.UK/UKCAT-TEST

UKCAT Marking

The UKCAT is marked based on the number of correct responses you give on the test. The test doesn't use negative marking. That means your score does not go down if you give a wrong answer, but instead you just fail to gain on that particular question.

The number of correct responses in each subtest (except for the Situational Judgement subtest) is scaled into a mark ranging from 300 to 900. The total score for the entire test therefore ranges from 1200 - 3600.

Unlike the other subtests, you receive a band score in the Situational Judgement section. The bands reflect the degree to which your answers match the same answers determined by a panel of medical experts and are assessed from band 1 to Band 4.

Band 1 means that most of your answers were the same as the panel of medical experts; Band 4 means very few of your answers matched. Your goal is to match the answers of the panel.

Band 1 – Very Good

Band 2 – Good

Band 3 – OK

Band 4 – Poor

The UKCAT does not have a specific pass mark, and different universities have different opinions on what they consider to be a good UKCAT score.

How do universities use the UKCAT?

In order to set a target score you must first understand how your choices use the UKCAT. Each university within the UKCAT consortium independently decides the importance of the UKCAT score. There is significant variation in how the various universities use the exam during their selection process. There are categorically two main approaches used by universities:

'Cut-off' Approach

This is when a university sets a universal cut-off, it is the lowest possible score or band score a candidate must achieve to be considered for the next stage in the application process. Typically, a UKCAT cut-off is based on the overall score achieved in the exam. However, there are universities that have a minimum requirement for each individual subtest. At the time of writing this book, St George's, University of London required applicants to have a minimum of 500 in each section of the UKCAT.

Many universities that adopt this approach tend to review and set their cut-off scores annually once the testing cycle is over and applications are submitted. So there is no way of knowing the UKCAT cut-off for the year you apply. A bit frustrating I know but not to worry, with some digging, which I will share later in this chapter, you can get a rough idea on the score needed to be considered and increase the likelihood of being invited for an interview. Nowadays, there is an increasing number of universities considering the band score in the situational judgement subtest and setting a banding cut-off. Whilst some universities do not take the STJ section into consideration, there are some that place a significant amount of emphasis on it. At the time of writing this guide, universities such as Keele, Leicester and Nottingham did not further consider candidates with a band 4 in the STJ section. More popularly, the STJ band score can be used for 'borderline cases' – this is when a university has two candidates who achieve the same score, and they can only invite one to interview or make one an offer, then they might look at the Situational Judgement as a final tool in making their selection.

Ranking Approach

Universities that do not have a UKCAT cut-off tend to use a ranking or scoring system to shortlist applicants. This is usually when applicants are awarded points based on the outcome of their UKCAT score as well as the overall application. Students that achieve high scores receive more points than students with lower scores.

Most scoring systems take into account other parts of an application such as academics, personal statement and reference, which are awarded points to create a total score which is ranked against other competing applicants. At the time of writing, Hull York medical school for example, used a point-based ranking system taking into consideration applicants' total UKCAT score and GCSEs.

Other medical and dental schools such as University of Edinburgh, Queen Mary University of London and University of Warwick are some of the popular choices known to adopt this scoring approach as well. Each university has their own approach to using the points-based system and consider different factors of one's entire application. I recommend considering these types of universities if you do not perform particularly well in the UKCAT, as other elements of your application may help boost total points earned.

When I applied for Medicine in 2015, I looked into every medical school in the UK that require the UKCAT and created the table below. The table gives an overview of the approach respective universities used to assess the UKCAT the year I applied. I encourage you to do the same and look at how all medical or dental schools assess the UKCAT. You may need to refer back to this, depending on the outcome of your UKCAT Score.

University	Assessment Type
University of Aberdeen	Ranking
Barts	Cut-off
University of Birmingham	Ranking
Cardiff University	Ranking
University of Central Lancashire	Ranking
University of Dundee	Ranking
University of Durham	Ranking
University of East Anglia	Ranking
University of Edinburgh	Ranking
University of Exeter	Cut-off
University of Glasgow	Ranking
Hull York Medical School	Cut-off
Keele University	Ranking
King's College,	Ranking
University of Leicester	Ranking

University of Liverpool	Ranking
University of Manchester	Cut-off
University of Newcastle	Cut-off
University of Nottingham	Ranking
Plymouth University	Ranking
Queen's Mary, University of	Cut-off
University of Sheffield	Cut-off
University of Southampton	Cut-off
University of St Andrews	Ranking
St George's, University of London	Cut-off
University of Warwick	Cut-off

Please note the table above refers to when I applied in 2015 not for recent entry, some universities might have changed their approach to assessing the exam. For the latest information on how universities use the UKCAT, see the most recent guide released by the UKCAT consortium, you can find a download link on the blog:

WWW.THEUKCATBLOG.COM/HOW-UNIVERSITIES-USE-THE-UKCAT

Further Digging into How Your Choices Assess The UKCAT

For a majority of universities, you should be able to find information regarding how they use the UKCAT on their website. However, there are some cases where the information might not be so easy to find.

Just like in Jade's case, her first choice did not provide much information on their website, only that they "do not use a UKCAT cut-off". Unfortunately, this is not sufficient to help determine whether Jade's UKCAT score is good enough for applying. Another popular case is when a university claims that they do use a cut-off but further states that "cut-off is determined after the testing cycle, once applications are submitted"

. I remember stumbling upon these issues myself when I applied to Medicine. However, there are some resources you can use to assess whether your score is good enough and set a target score before taking the test; they are as follows:

1. Official UKCAT Score Guide

The UKCAT score guide is a document released by the UKCAT every year that provides an overview of how each university part of the consortium, uses the UKCAT during their admission process. The document tries to provide up to date information directly copied from the university website. For each university, the document includes a retrieval date i.e. the date that the information was cited on the university's website. To reduce the likelihood for any omissions, inaccuracies or changes, the document also includes links to the university websites where information is cited for you to check again. There is always a chance a university may make some changes so I encourage going through the links provided.

You can find a download link to the latest version of the score guide on the blog at:

WWW.THEUKCATBLOG.COM/HOW-UNIVERSITIES-USE-THE-UKCAT

I recommend going through the following points when using the document to research universities:

- Is there a minimum UKCAT requirement?
- If there is no cut-off, how are applicants ranked?
- How much emphasis is put on the other parts of an application?
- Is the Situational Judgement taken into consideration? If so, at what stage.

2. Admissions Office

Every medical and dental school has an admissions team responsible for managing admission for their respective courses. They are generally very helpful and can provide valuable information not included on the university website. However, do note that at times they most likely will not give much information regarding how they assess the UKCAT the year you are applying. However, you are more likely to get information about previous application cycles. I remember when I applied the third time I was so 'desperate' that I called the respective admission teams to get more insight into their application process. If the tutor on the phone did not know the answer to my question, I followed up with an email. In some cases, I called again to follow up when I got no answer.

Below are a few questions that worked really well:

- Did you have a UKCAT cut-off last year?

- How is the UKCAT cut-off determined?

- What was the UKCAT cut-off last year?

- How much emphasis was put on the UKCAT last year?

- Did you use a ranking system last year?

- How was the UKCAT assessed last year?

- What would you say is a good UKCAT score?

- How did you rank applicants last year?

- I understand you use a point-based system to rank applicants, how are the points determined?

- How many students applied last year and how many did you invite for interview?

- How many places do you have on your course?

I discovered that I got more information asking direct questions like "What was the UKCAT score cut-off last year?" than generic questions like "What is a good UKCAT score?". I noticed admission tutors responded better to questions that showed I've done a bit of research before calling

For example, "I understand you use a point-based system to rank applicants, how are the points determined?". When you begin to look into how universities assess the UKCAT, I strongly recommend you record your findings as you may need to refer back to it from time to time. I recorded mine on an Excel spreadsheet and found this very convenient for referring back to when I had to shortlist my choices down to 4.

Now let's take a deeper dive at some of the questions that worked really well when I called the admissions office. I want to explain their significance and how you can use the information to set a target score:

1. Did you use a UKCAT cut-off last year?

For universities that do not provide much information on their websites, I found this question extremely helpful. The last thing you want is to be applying to a university with a UKCAT score below their cut-off. This question is great because it is closed and the tutor only has two options to respond - Yes or No. If they respond with Yes, record it on a table, as seen below, that they use a 'cut-off'. If NO, record it as 'ranking'. Great follow up questions if it is a YES —"Great! What was the cut-off last year?" and record the response. Always seek to ask additional questions that will help mould out a rough estimate for the score you need. If the tutor doesn't seem sure or has no clue, politely ask for their name and email address then immediately send an email to follow up. Highly unlikely but if for whatever reason they refuse to provide an answer, I recommend calling back and rephrasing your question, something like "What was the minimum UKCAT score for candidates you invited for interview last year?" or perhaps "What is a good UKCAT score?".

Below is the list of universities that used a cut-off the year I applied, ranked from lowest to highest. Please note that some of the cut-off scores are estimates based on calls with the admissions office or information from their website. Also note that this may mostly likely not be the same for the year you apply.

University	Cur-off Score
Barts	2400
Hull York	2400
Exeter	2500
Southampton	2500
St Georges	2590
Sheffield	2600
Warwick	2690
Newcastle / Durham	2718
Manchester	2810
King's College	2920

2. Did you use a ranking system last year?

This is another great closed question for universities that may award points. Great follow up questions include "Which components of an application is ranked/scored?" or "Which component holds most weight on total score?". The key thing you want to know is how points are awarded and which component is the most important factor, universities that use a ranking system where they factor other parts of your application may be a better consideration if you do not perform particularly well in the UKCAT. Take note that some ranking universities place a lot of emphasis on the UKCAT. At the time of writing this book, King's College University of London mentioned the UKCAT as the most important factor when shortlisting applicants - these types of universities might be better applying to if you don't have particularly strong academics but have achieved a high UKCAT score. At the same time, there were universities that did not put much emphasis on the UKCAT, like the University of Aberdeen that used a score ranking system where the UKCAT accounted for 40% and academics accounted for 60%.

3. Did you consider the band score in Situational Judgement last year?

The Situational Judgement is the final subtest of the UKCAT. Unlike the other sections, you do not receive a score out of 900. Instead, you are assessed from Band 1 (Very Good) to Band 4 (Poor). The section measures your ability to understand real world situations and identify critical factors and appropriate behaviour in dealing with them. Some universities such as Keele, Nottingham and Liverpool consider this section of the exam and automatically reject candidates with a band 4 score. Whilst others such as Warwick and Southampton did not even consider this section at the time of writing this guide. Even If you achieve a high UKCAT score but end up with a band 3 or 4 in the STJ section, I wouldn't advise applying to a university that considers the STJ section, chances are, you'll get rejected.

4. How many students applied last year and how many places do you have on your course?

To help measure the 'competitiveness' of a course, I asked the above question to create an **Applicants to Places** ratio. The ratio is a measure of how competitive a course is based on how many students apply versus the number of places on the course. Let's take another look at the universities that used a cut-off when I applied and rank them according to 'competitiveness' using this ratio.

	Cut-off	No of Applications	Places	Application: Places Ratio
St George's	2590	1000	135	7.4
Manchester	2810	3000	380	7.9
Bart's	2400	2369	260	9.1
Newcastle	2718	3000	327	9.2
Sheffield	2600	2500	237	10.5

Kings	2920	3500	330	10.6
Hull York	2400	1400	130	10.8
Exeter	2500	1700	130	13.1
Southampton	2500	4000	276	14.5
Warwick	2690	3000	164	18.3

From the table above we can deduce that for St George's, about 7 people were applying for every place, for Manchester that about 8 people were applying for every place, Bart's about 9 people were applying for every place and so on.

Let's assume I achieved a score of 2600 when I took the test, then the following "cut-off' universities would be the ones I would consider:

University	Cut-off	Applications: Places
Barts	2400	9.1
Hull York	2400	10.8
Exeter	2500	13.1
Southampton	2500	14.5
St Georges	2590	7.4
Sheffield	2600	10.5

At first glance, you might be thinking that applying to Barts or Hull York would be the best options as they have the lowest cut-off scores, but when you consider the application to places ratio are they the best options? Take into consideration Hull York for example, it is far more competitive than applying to St Georges and Sheffield. Therefore, all things considered, Hull York might not be a great choice despite the low UKCAT requirement.

The Application:Places ratio approach is flawed in some parts as it doesn't really tell you about the real nature of the competitive selection process at each university. I recommend that you choose a medical or dental school based largely on its course structure, its teaching style and whether you have a strong chance of getting in. However, working out the Application:Places ratio can be an additional factor to help with shortlisting choices, especially when you have to pick between two choices with similar requirements.

Last Piece of The Puzzle

Once you understand how universities use the UKCAT, use results from your research to set a target score. Your UKCAT target score is the minimum score you need to achieve to apply to your ideal choices, not factoring other parts of your application, it is the minimum score needed to increase the likelihood of being invited for an interview or being offered a place.

I appreciate you want to score as high as possible in the exam but setting a minimum target score beforehand helps with assessing your performance as you prepare for the exam.

Target Score = UKCAT Cut-off For #1 Choice

If your first choice uses a UKCAT cut-off, set your target practice score as this minimum. For universities that use a ranking system or are not clear about how they use the UKCAT, I recommend giving them a call to get a rough estimate. If that proves futile, use the UKCAT statistics released by the exam board each year.

The UKCAT uses a statistical approach called decile to report the overall performance of candidates each year.

A decile is any of the nine values that divide a data into ten equal parts so that each part represents 10% of the sample population.

This statistical approach is descriptive and gives a good overview of the overall UKCAT performance each year. The highest scoring applicants will be in the 9th decile while the lowest scoring candidates will be in the 1st decile. Universities analyse the official UKCAT results and compare them with their applicant pool. When setting my target score, I used the decile ranges from the previous year, the 2014 UKCAT results, to set a minimum target practice score for universities that used a ranking approach.

Decile	2014 Results (Out of 3600)
1st	2210
2nd	2330
3rd	2410
4th	2470
5th	2540
6th	2600
7th	2660
8th	2740
9th	2840

The total score for each decile indicates the score a candidate can achieve to be classified in that decile. For example, in 2014, a candidate score from 2540 to 2599 would be in the 5th decile, and a candidate score from 2840 upwards would be in the 9th decile.

The overall UKCAT performance is released by the exam board after each testing cycle and can be found on the official UKCAT website. You can find the deciles and mean scores from previous years on my blog:

WWW. THEUKCATBLOG.COM/UKCAT-MEAN-SCORES-DECILES/

Use the UKCAT results from the previous year to set a target score if your first choice uses a ranking system. In some cases, where your first choice does provide information on how they rank applicants, I suggest using their formulae to set a target score. The decile approach should only be used if your first choice does not provide much information or if it is suggested that the UKCAT is the main component when ranking candidates.

Based on my research in 2015, I decided to set a minimum practice target score of 2600 which was the minimum score for the 6th decile in 2014. After looking into my ideal 4 choices I set my ideal target score to 2800 (i.e. 700 in each section).

IDEAL SCORE – 2800

(Based on Researching Ideal Choices)

MINIMUM - 2600

(Based on Researching Previous year results)

Generally, scores in the 6th decile, i.e. the top 40%, are typically considered to be good UKCAT scores. However, this doesn't mean that if you achieve below this you will not get a place into medicine or dentistry, you may just need to consider universities that do not rely so heavily on the UKCAT.

During practice tests and mocks, you will aim to achieve the target score set. This score will help with gauging your performance during practice. We will discuss this in more detail in the 'Assess' chapter of this guide.

Please note it is possible that the cut-off for your first choice might be below the 6th decile for the previous year. If this is the case I recommend setting the decile score as the ideal and the university's cut-off as the minimum target score.

Before we move into the second step of the strategy, have an ideal and minimum UKCAT target score set. You will refer back to these scores as you prepare for the UKCAT. Now let's identify your weakest areas and create an attack plan to boost both skill and familiarity with the exam.

BONUS EXERCISE!

Sharing is a great way to stay motivated and hold yourself accountable. If you're on Twitter or Instagram, I'd love to see a picture or video of how your UKCAT preparation is coming along.

Use the hashtag **#UKCATStudyGuide**, and if you want to make sure I see it, also include **@theukcatblog**, somewhere in your message.

I look forward to seeing you take charge of your UKCAT preparation, and feel free to click on the hashtag to see other candidates taking charge too!

Step 2: Identify

Identifying Your Weakest Areas

The subtest you identify as weakest will ultimately define how you tailor the rest of the strategy. Identifying and focussing on weak areas is a bullet-proof way to significantly increase your total UKCAT score. However, with so many resources available, it can be confusing and difficult to know where to start. In this chapter I'll show you step-by-step, how to identify your weakest section and discover which element you struggle with the most.

The TWO main mistakes most candidates make during this step is firstly they assume the subtest they score the lowest is their weakest. Secondly, once they have falsely identified this weakness they would attempt more practice questions instead of more targeted study that involves analysing question-types and reasoning skill. For instance, let's assume a candidate discovered that the abstract reasoning section was their weakness, they could practice general questions to improve

. However, the abstract section has 4 different question-types. Depending on their shortcomings, a more effective approach would be identifying which question-type the candidate struggles with the most and practice more of this specific type. Another approach could be honing their technique for spotting patterns. Both approaches are far more effective in improving one's overall abstract score than attempting more general questions.

So before we begin to identify your weakest section let's take a deeper look into the tasks, question-types and skills being tested in each section. It is important to know this to effectively identify the areas to work on.

Verbal Reasoning - Task, Question-types & Skills

The verbal reasoning section assesses your ability to read and think carefully about the information presented in passages and to determine whether specific conclusions can be drawn from information presented. You are not expected to use prior knowledge to answer the questions - for example, it the text states that London is the capital of France, you need to 'believe' this statement when you use the passage to determine the correct answer. The verbal subtest includes two main types of questions:

- True/False/Can't Tell

- Comprehension Type

True/False/Can't Tell - You are required to read a passage of text. Following this, you are presented with statements. For each statement you must decide if, based on the passage of text, it is true, false or you cannot tell if it is true or false.

Comprehension Type - Following each passage, you are presented with four questions or incomplete statements. You must then choose which of four free text answers applies.

This question type assesses critical thinking abilities, such as identifying conclusions and proving causality. They include - incomplete statements, according to the passage, except question and most likely questions.

With both question-types you have to read the text provided, think carefully about the information presented, and use the information to answer each item. The following skills are being tested in the Verbal Reasoning Section:

- Comprehension

- Critical Thinking

- Speed

Comprehension: This is your ability in understanding and interpreting of what is being read. If you find yourself getting a majority of questions wrong because you misunderstood the passage, then this is probably a weakness. We will cover tips and strategies to boost comprehension skills later in the guide.

Critical Thinking: Some questions may require you to make inferences and draw conclusions from different parts of the passage. If you find this difficult then you may need to work on critical thinking. I must admit this was a weakness of mine when it came to the verbal section; we will cover tips for improving critical thinking when preparing for the verbal section.

Speed: You have 21 minutes to answer 44 questions, that's about 30 seconds per question! If, during practice, you find yourself not finishing the section in time then this probably is a weakness. We will take a look at time-saving strategies and tips for improving speed.

Decision Making - Task, Question-types & Skills

The Decision-Making subtest tests your ability to apply logic to reach a decision or conclusion, evaluate arguments and analyse statistical information. The Decision-Making question-types are not as straightforward as the verbal section; instead candidates can expect numerous question-types broken down in the type of skill being tested. The Decision-Making subtest tests four main skills, they are as follows:

- Deductive Reasoning

- Evaluating Arguments

- Statistical Reasoning

- Speed

Deductive Reasoning: This is your process of reasoning from one or more statements to reach a logically certain conclusion. In the test, you will be presented with items that are in the form of syllogism or logical puzzles.

- Syllogism: These are questions where a conclusion is drawn from two given or assumed propositions (premises); a common or middle term is present in the two premises but not in the conclusion, which may be invalid (e.g. all dogs are animals; all animals have four legs; therefore, all dogs have four legs. If you are getting these types of questions wrong, then this is an area for improvement.

- Logical Puzzles: The UKCAT also includes puzzles where statements are provided, and you have to piece together what is happening. This involves clear and logical thinking.

Evaluating Arguments: The Decision-Making section also includes questions that assess your ability to evaluate arguments. These types of questions usually account for 35% of the real test. They are in the form of two question types:

- Recognising assumptions: These types of questions are typically standalone statements where you'll be will have four answer options.

- Interpreting information and drawing a conclusion: These types of questions typically involve a graph, chart or table where you will be given 5 statements and be required to respond to each statement by placing a 'yes' or 'no' answer next to each statement.

Statistical Reasoning: These are questions that require some degree of mathematical skills; they test the ability to assess probability and deal with statistical information. There are two subtypes:

- Venn Diagrams: A Venn diagram is a diagram that shows all possible logical relations between a finite collection of different sets. You should be aware of this from GCSE's, the UKCAT has incorporated this into the DM subtest.

- Probability: The other type of statistical reasoning question, Probability, is about estimating how likely (probable) something is to happen. The DM section includes probability questions that require candidates to select a response from four options.

Speed: You have 31 minutes to complete 29 items, that's just over 1 minute per question. It might seem like a lot of time compared to the verbal section but bear in mind you have to read statements and constantly re-evaluate the options provided.

Quantitative Reasoning - Task, Question-types & Skills

The Quantitative Reasoning subtest assesses your ability to use numerical skills to solve problems by extracting relevant information from tables and other numerical presentations. Question-types come in many forms, usually in the form of tables and graphs. The subtest involves two main skills:

Numerical problem-solving skills: This is a measure of your numerical ability in evaluating and deducing data to solve problems. The subtest assumes you have familiarity with core GCSE concepts.

You'll be expected to solve problems by reviewing graphs, tables and other types of information.

Speed: You have 24 minutes to answer 36 questions! It might seem impossible to cover all the questions in that time, I will run through time-saving strategies and techniques later.

Abstract Reasoning - Task, Question-types & Skills

The Abstract Reasoning section assesses your ability to identify patterns amongst abstract shapes. There are four different types of questions in this section, they include:

Type 1 - You are presented with two sets of shapes labelled "Set A" and "Set B". You will be given a test shape and asked to decide whether the test shape belongs to Set A, Set B, or Neither.

Type 2 - You are presented with a series of shapes. You will be asked to select the next shape in the series.

Type 3 - You are presented with a statement, involving a group of shapes. You will be asked to determine which shape completes the statement.

Type 4 - You are presented with two sets of shapes labelled "Set A" and "Set B". You will be asked to select which of the four response options belongs to Set A or Set B.

The abstract reasoning section tests your pattern-finding skills and speed, where you have 24 minutes to answer 36 questions.

Situational Judgement - Task, Question-types & Skills

The Situational Judgement test measures your capacity to understand real world situations and how to identify critical factors and appropriate behaviour in dealing with them.

Unlike the other subtests, you do not receive a score out of 900 in the real test. Instead you are assessed from Band 1 to Band 4. A band 1 is very good whilst a Band 4 score is poor. In the situational judgement test there are two types of questions tested, they include:

- **Appropriateness Questions**: This usually account for roughly 60% of the items. This is where you are given a scenario and presented with an action. You will need to rate how appropriate this action is in the context of the scenario. You are given four answer choices to choose from, they include:

- **A very appropriate thing to do** - if it will address at least one aspect (not necessarily all aspects) of the situation.
- **Appropriate, but not ideal** – if it could be done, but is not necessarily a very good thing to do
- **Inappropriate, but not awful** – if it should not really be done, but would not be terrible
- **A very inappropriate thing to do** – if it should definitely not be done and would make the situation worse

- **Importance Questions:** This accounts for the remaining 40% of the items. This is where after each scenario you are presented with an action. You must rate how important it is to carry out that action in the context of the scenario. Those actions which are considered essential should be awarded high importance. If an action is inconsequential, or even detrimental, then it will be of lower importance, you are given four answer choices to choose from, they include:

- **Very important** – if this is something that is vital to take into account
- **Important** – if this is something that is important but not vital to take into account
- **Of minor importance** – if this is something that could be taken into account, but it does not matter if it is considered or not
- **Not important at all** – if this is something that should definitely not be taken into account.

<u>Take note</u> of the question-types in each subtest, we will refer back to this as we try to identify weak areas in the exam and develop an effective strategy to target each section.

Attempting the Official UKCAT Resources

There are so many commercial resources available that advise on how to pass the UKCAT. The problem is that the UKCAT does not work with any of them, so you potentially run the risk of spending a lot of money on irrelevant or dated material. However, a survey conducted by the UKCAT does prove that using these unofficial books, courses or seminars are associated with higher overall performance. The only official resources are on the UKCAT website, we will use these resources to identify your true weakness.

The preparation tools provided on the UKCAT website are extremely helpful. The exam board covers a variety of topics ranging from test strategies to candidate advice as well as tips for preparing for the test. I recommended you go through all the resources available on their website. The first exercise in identifying your weakest skill involves using the official practice tests and practice questions they provide.

<u>WWW.UKCAT.AC.UK/UKCAT-TEST/UKCAT-PREPARATION/</u>

In my first attempt at the UKCAT, I did the official practice tests at the end of my preparation; I thought it would give me a rough idea of what my score would be in the actual exam. In hindsight, this was a bad idea because I achieved a poor score and it was too late to improve my skills. I discovered this is also a common mistake made by applicants. The practice tests and questions are the only official resources available so I recommend taking advantage of this early on.

They are updated every year to reflect the same level of difficulty candidates will encounter in the exam. The first step in identifying your weakness is attempting the official practice questions and tests.

The first exercise in identifying your weakness involves attempting the official question banks for each subtest untimed. You will need a pen and notebook to make notes as you attempt questions.

Exercise 1: Attempt Official UKCAT Questions Banks Untimed

The UKCAT provides practice questions for each subtest: Verbal reasoning, Decision Making, Quantitative Reasoning, Abstract Reasoning and Situational Judgement. Attempt each set of practice questions untimed. The aim of this is to familiarise yourself with each section of the exam; do not practice any questions beforehand nor worry about time management. If it takes you a whole day to go through the entire set of practice questions that's fine. It's not a race, attempt each set and take notes of the question-types you found difficult.

> Use the Official Question Banks to familiarise yourself with the exam. Do no studying beforehand nor worry about time management. The whole point is to familiarize yourself with the exam.

Verbal Reasoning Question Banks

Go through the question banks provided untimed and review your answers at the end. I recommend taking note of question-types you find difficult and learn from the solutions afterwards.

After you have completed the verbal question banks and reviewed answers, try to reflect on the entire test and think about what you struggled with the most. Do not get too caught up in specifics for now, try to identify which of the skills being tested you could improve:

- Comprehension

- Critical Thinking
- Speed

The table below provides assistance to help identify which skill might need improvement:

Critical Thinking	Comprehension	Speed
Drawing false conclusions Making wrong inferences	Misunderstanding passage Guessing answer options. Making assumptions Poor Retention: Cannot remember topic for each paragraph.	Reading text one word at a time Vocalising while reading: Reading words out loud. Regressing: regularly going back to reread words or sentences

When I attempted the verbal question bank, I struggled on speed and critical thinking, I was also a slow reader without realising it. I would constantly regress and at times vocalise. This significantly reduced my reading speed and level of comprehension. Identifying this early on enabled me to adopt strategies to improve and ultimately increase my verbal score in the UKCAT. Try to spot which element you struggle with the most and write it down.

Decision Making Question Banks

Go through the question banks provided untimed and review your answers at the end. I recommend taking note of question-types you find difficult and learn from the solutions afterwards.

After you have completed the Decision-making question banks and reviewed the answers, reflect on the entire test and think about which skill you struggled with the most:

- Deductive Reasoning
- Evaluating Arguments
- Statistical Reasoning
- Speed

The table below provides assistance to help identify areas for improvement:

Deductive	Evaluating	Statistical
Struggle on puzzle questions Not recognising links between different information Making wrong assumptions	Mis-interpreting graphs and charts. Misinterpreting information from problems in text.	Poor grasp of Venn diagram Poor grasp of key probability concepts

Speed
Spending too much time on a question
Reading text one word at a time
Hyper Regressing: going back to reread words or sentences regularly

Quantitative Reasoning Question Banks

Go through the question banks provided untimed and review your answers at the end. I recommend taking note of topics you find difficult and learn from the solutions afterwards.

To do well in the quantitative reasoning subtest, you need to be familiar with some basic mathematical operations, which you may already know from GCSE level mathematics:

- Addition, subtraction, multiplication and division
- Percentages, ratios and fractions
- Speed, distance and time calculations
- Working with money
- Areas and volumes
- Graphs and chart

You may notice you feel rusty on some topics. Take note of them. Another thing to take note is the format of questions, for instance, items in this section are presented in the form of tables, charts and graphs. Were you able to rapidly identify relevant information from the presentation? If not, then you may need to work on numerical speed as well.

The table below provides assistance to help identify areas of improvement:

Numerical Skills	Speed
Slow to perform simple mathematical operations	Spending too much time on an item
Cannot convert from one measurement to another	Not using onscreen calculator efficiently
Struggle to apply different kinds of averages	Reading text one word at a time

Uncomfortable with fractions and decimals	Hyper-Regressing: going back to reread words or sentences regularly
Slow to solve basic equations	
Mis-interpret proportions, percentages and ratios.	Obsessing over exact answer. Not estimating and eliminating.

Abstract Reasoning Question Bank

Go through the question banks provided untimed and review your answers at the end. I recommend taking note of which of the 4 question types you find difficult and learn from the solutions afterwards.

The abstract reasoning sections test your pattern-finding skills and speed. You rarely notice pattern similarity instantly. With enough practice you will improve, the more questions you practice, the easier you'll find the subtest. Do not get dispirited if you struggle with it. We will cover pattern finding strategies later in this guide, but for now, work at your own pace, try to think of your own best approach to answering questions and use the following list of ideas to focus on the commonality within each set:

- Shape of components
- Number of corners on each component
- Type of edges on each component
- Colour of each component
- Number of components
- Orientation of components
- Consistent (or consistently evolving) position of one component relative to the others
- Size of components

The above suggestions are a good starting point. By applying this list of possibilities to each set, you can improve generating hypothesis and spot the patterns quicker. The table below provides assistance to help identify areas of improvement:

Abstract Skills	Speed
Slow or unable to spot pattern commonality	Spending too much time on an item
Not wary of red herrings	Not using flagging system

Situational Judgement Question Banks

The Situational Judgement section (STJ) is different from the other subtests; technically there is no right or wrong answer when you think about how it is marked. My advice would be to take note of which of the two question-types you struggle with the most and carefully monitor speed, you should notice a pattern.

After you have attempted the STJ practice questions and reviewed the answers, learn from the answer rationale provided by the UKCAT. I'll show you how I was able to improve my Situational Judgement band score later in this book, for now only review answers and learn from them.

Review your notes for each subtest before moving to the next exercise, propose solutions of your own and try to implement them for the next exercise. There is no need to do any further practice or refer to any other resource at this time.

Exercise 2 - Attempt the Official UKCAT Practice Tests Timed

The UKCAT provides three UKCAT practice tests, you will attempt all three tests under timed conditions. There is no need to dive into books or courses at this stage. You have familiarised yourself with the exam by going through the practice questions in the question banks, now you must mimic the testing conditions and identify which sections are your weakest.

Each test is about 2 hours long so I recommend doing one practice test a day and reviewing your answers afterwards on the same day. For example, if you take Practice Test A on Day 1, review your answers afterwards, then attempt Practice Test B on Day 2 and so on. I recommend this approach because the test is really exhausting. When you are attempting a practice test, treat it like the real exam, try to mimic the same environment. Make sure you are in a quiet place and be sure you won't be disturbed the entire 2 hours you are taking the test. The whole point of this is to give you first-hand experience of the time limitations in each section of the exam and identify the part of the exams you find difficult with no practice.

Once you have gone through the official practice questions and familiarised yourself with the exam, attempt all three official practice tests under timed conditions with no prior studying. This is the most effective way to identify where your natural capabilities lie.

Exercise 3 - Review Your Practice Test Scores

Once you have completed a practice test, you will be taken to a Review Screen - this screen shows your score in each section. Spend time reviewing the questions in each section, do not just go through the items you got wrong, understand the answers for every question. There is an "explain answer" button for each question on the top left-hand corner; by clicking on this you will obtain an explanation as to the correct answer.

Understand the explanations and take note of the question-types you got wrong and those you luckily got right. For instance, you might realise that you didn't do well on logical puzzles in the Decision-Making subtest but quite well on the Venn diagram questions. This suggests you will need to practice more logical puzzles to boost your overall Decision-Making score.

You also want to reflect on your use of time in each subtest as well, did you finish each section in time? If not, why? Did you rush towards the end in a specific section? If so, why? Before learning any of the strategies recommended in this guide, try to propose solutions of your own and try to implement them for the remaining practice tests.

To summarise, make sure after each practice test to do the following:

- Understand the explained answers for ALL items (you might have fluked a few).
- Identify the specific question-type in each section you find most difficult.
- Reflect on your use of time.

Exercise 4 - Calculate Practice Test Scores

After you've completed a practice test, you will notice that the final review screen doesn't give a score out of 900 in each section. Instead, you are provided with the total number of incorrect responses in each section. You can simply calculate the number of correct responses achieved by subtracting the number of incorrect responses from the total number of items in each subtest, for example, if the review screen states you achieved 11 incorrect responses in the verbal reasoning section then you scored 33 out of 44. Record the number of correct responses for each section and put into the format of the table below.

	Practice Test A	Practice Test B	Practice Test C	Average Score
Verbal Reasoning (out of 44)				
Decision Making (out of 29)				

Quantitative Reasoning (out of 36)				
Abstract Reasoning (out of 55)				

Please note that the Situational Judgement scores are not included in our calculation. This is due to the fact that your score in this section will not count towards your overall test score out of 3600. Instead you'll be given a band score from 1 to 4.

Once you've recorded your scores as seen above, the next step is to convert the **average score** in each section into an approximate UKCAT score out of 900 using the conversion table on my blog (or on pg 204).

WWW.THEUKCATBLOG.COM/UKCAT-CONVERSION-TABLE/

Please note that the conversion table is for approximation purposes only. Scores on the UKCAT are given in 10-point intervals, so actual scores will vary slightly. This table is designed to bark on the side of caution, so in most cases, a similar performance on the UKCAT would result in a slightly higher score.

Using the conversion table, record your average score in each subtest out of 900 as seen in the table below.

	Average Score (Out of 900)
Verbal Reasoning	
Quantitative Reasoning	
Abstract Reasoning	
Decision Making	

Quick Note: Your practice test scores will most likely be really low at this stage - do not panic, it's expected since you have done no preparation.

Exercise 5 - Use UKCAT Results to Identify 'True' Weakness

As you are now aware, the UKCAT uses a statistical approach called deciles to report the overall performance of candidates each year. It is any of the nine values that divide the UKCAT results into ten equal parts so that each part represents 10% of the sample population. This statistical approach is descriptive and gives a good overview of the overall test performance each year. Each decile represents 10% of the total candidates based on their overall test performance.

The total score for each decile indicates the highest score a candidate can achieve to be classified in that decile. For example, in 2015 (the year I took the exam), a candidate that achieved 2540 would be in the 5th decile and a candidate score at 2840 would be in the 9th decile. The term percentile can also be used instead of decile, which means out of 100, for instance, a score in the 1st decile represents a score at the 10th percentile; the 2nd decile represents a score at the 20th percentile, and so on. You can find the latest result statistics on the official UKCAT website, I've provided a summary of the average UKCAT scores from 2012 to date in the article below.

WWW.THEUKCATBLOG.COM/WHAT-IS-THE-AVERAGE-UKCAT-SCORE

The data provided by the UKCAT is valuable because you can compare your practice test scores to the UKCAT score in the previous cycle. Take a look at the practice test results in the table below. It is the practice result from Natacha, a family friend and previous medicine applicant, that I taught my preparation strategy in 2016.

	Average Score (Out of 900)
Verbal Reasoning	
Quantitative Reasoning	
Abstract Reasoning	
Decision Making	

*Please note that the Decision-Making section is a relatively new subtest, it was introduced in the 2016 testing cycle. As a result, overall test scores in 2016 was out of 2700 instead of 3600.

You are probably at this point thinking that Natacha's weakest section is verbal reasoning because it is her lowest score. However, when compared to the official UKCAT results from the previous year, it reveals a whole different picture. The table below compares her practice score with the previous year averages in each section.

When compared to last year's result, Natacha scored above average in verbal reasoning and below average in the other two sections. Using basic statistics which we will dive into in the next chapter, we can conclude that Natacha's strongest section is the verbal reasoning subtest and her weakest section is the quantitative section. The key thing to take from this is that your lowest score isn't necessarily your weakest section. This is one of the most common mistakes made by candidates when preparing for the exam; they assume their lowest score is their weakest and spend more time trying to improve this 'false weakness'.

	Average Practice Score (out of 900)	2015 UKCAT Averages
Verbal Reasoning	580	577

Quantitative Reasoning	624	685
Abstract Reasoning	610	640

Table comparing Natacha's practice tests results with previous year.

Compare your practice test results with the previous year average. If your average in a subtest is below last year's average consider it weak, if it's above, consider it strong

Once you have completed all five exercises, you should have a rough idea where your natural capabilities lie and be able to identify your weakest and strongest subtests. If you have scored below the previous year averages in all four subtests, do not worry, it's expected. I will run through how to spot your true weakness and prioritise each subtest in the next chapter. For those that have scored above the average scores from the previous year in all sections good work! Regardless, you still need to identify your true weakness. The next part of my strategy will help with prioritising each subtest and determining the amount of time to spend preparing for each section.

Step 3: Prioritise

Prioritising the UKCAT Subtests

One afternoon during my final year at university, I was sitting in the middle of my Neuropharmacology lecture when my phone's vibration went crazy. I was included in a trend on The Student Room Forum where a candidate wanted to know the amount of practice time he should spend on each section of the exam. The trend was read by thousands of students and lead to a lot of replies to the post. After my lecture, I had a look at the responses, there were a few good tips from other students but a lot of really bad ones. The following bad ones stood out to me the most:

- Spend a majority of time on the subtest you score in the lowest
- You only need 3 - 4 weeks to prepare, practice as many questions as possible within that time and you'll be fine

They are common mistakes candidates make when prioritising the UKCAT subtests. Firstly, candidates assume that the section where they achieve the lowest score is their weakest subtest. Secondly, candidates can at times fall into the trap of spending too much time on sections of the exam they find most comfortable, sometimes without even realising it. These two problems create the necessity of this step, to help Prioritise each section and manage time appropriately.

Bad Advice #1 - Spend a majority of time on the subtest you score the lowest

This is really bad advice, determining the order of dealing with the UKCAT subtests is important because it mostly defines the amount of practice time you will allocate to each section. I recommend spending the majority of time focusing on your weakest section; it is the most effective way to significantly increase your total UKCAT score. However, your lowest score isn't necessarily your weakest; it is common for candidates to assume their lowest score is their weakest. Let's take another look Natacha's practice results, the family friend I taught my preparation strategy back in 2016.

	Natacha's Average Practice Score (out of 900)
Verbal Reasoning	580
Quantitative Reasoning	610
Abstract Reasoning	624
Decision Making*	N/A

*Please note that the Decision-Making section is a relatively new subtest, it was introduced in the 2016 testing cycle. As a result, overall test scores in 2016 were out of 2700 instead of 3600.

Also note that I have chosen to ignore the situational judgment section as it does not contribute to the overall UKCAT score, you will be given a separate band score.

You immediately assume her weakest section is the verbal section because it's her lowest score. However, when compared to the previous year, she scored above average and it is in fact her strongest section.

I use Natacha's practice result to explain this concept because it's a great example as her highest scoring section was her weakest and her lowest scoring subtest was her strongest.

	Average Practice Score (out of 900)	2015 UKCAT Averages
Verbal Reasoning	580	577
Quantitative Reasoning	624	685
Abstract Reasoning	610	640

When I took the official practice tests in 2015, I compared my score to the 2014 averages, the table below shows how my practice score compared:

	My Average Practice Score (out of 900)	2014 UKCAT Averages (out of 900)
Verbal Reasoning	527	571
Quantitative Reasoning	640	684
Abstract Reasoning	680	636
Decision Analysis*	585	614

*Please note that the Decision Analysis subtest no longer features in the UKCAT test, it has been replaced with the Decision-Making Subtest.

As you can see my average UKCAT practice score in the verbal, quantitative and decision analysis sections were below average. The only section I scored above average was in abstract reasoning. From this, I concluded my strongest section was abstract reasoning. The next part was identifying the order of weakness with respect to the previous year.

Determining the Order to Deal with Each Subtest

Exercise 1 - Calculate Percentage Difference

In some cases, it might not be as easy to spot your weakest or strongest section. For example, candidates that score below average on all four sections or even above average in all sections. Calculating the percentage difference between your score and the official averages gives a good indication of the extent of your skill, which we will use to identify your true weakness and rank the subtests in order. Find the formulae for calculating percentage difference below:

$$P.D = \frac{Practice\ score - Last\ Year\ Score}{Last\ Year\ Score} \times 100$$

Use the formulae above to calculate the percentage difference for each subtest.

Example:

Average Practice VR score achieved = 527, Last Year VR Average= 571

$$P.D = \frac{527 - 571}{571} \times 100$$

Percentage difference = -7.7% i.e. **7.7% below last year's average**

The table below shows the percentage difference of my practice score and the UKCAT averages in 2014 to give an indication the extent of my skill.

I scored 7.7% below the previous year in Verbal Reasoning, which suggests that the subtest is my weakest section. Quantitative Reasoning came in second at 6.9% below previous average and Decision Analysis as my third weakest (or second strongest) subtest at 4.7% below the average.

In a nutshell, the UKCAT section with the largest percentage difference below the previous average is considered the weakest section and the section with the largest percentage difference above average is considered strongest.

This technique is great because if you achieve below (or above) the average UKCAT scores in all sections, you can still identify and rank your weakest sections accordingly.

	Average Practice Score (out of 900)	2014 Averages (out of 900)	Percentage difference
Verbal Reasoning	527	571	**-7.7 %**
Quantitative Reasoning	640	684	**-6.4%**
Abstract Reasoning	680	636	**+6.9%**
Decision Analysis	585	614	**-4.7%**

Calculate the percentage difference between your practice score and the UKCAT scores for each subtest. You can find the latest averages at the official UKCAT website or summary of the results on the blog at:

Exercise 2 - Create A Priority Table (Optional)

I believe calculating the percentage difference between your practice score and the previous year's results is an effective way to rank subtests based on weakness. Once you've worked out the differences for each subtest, create a priority table showing the order of priority for each section and the minimum amount of hours you plan to spend on it subtest. The figure below shows my priority table when preparing for the UKCAT back in 2015.

Subtest	Strength	Priority
Verbal Reasoning	Weakest	1st
Quantitative Reasoning	2nd Weakest	2nd
Decision Analysis*	2nd Strongest	3rd
Abstract Reasoning	Strongest	4th

The table shows my weakest (highest priority) to strongest (least priority). I arranged the subtests in order of priority based on the results from calculating the percentage difference. I strongly recommend spending the majority of your time improving your weakest subtest i.e. the UKCAT section with the largest percentage difference below average. Studies have shown that more time spent on strong areas improves overall test mark by an average of 10 to 15 percent while more time spent on weakest areas can improve overall test score by 20 to 35 percent - That is an extra 180 points in each UKCAT subtest by simply focusing on weak areas.

Bad advice #2 - You only need 3- 4 weeks to prepare, practice as many questions as possible within that time and you'll be fine.

This is more bad advice that provides no structure to preparation and doesn't take into account that every candidate is different. The following exercises will help you with determining how long to prepare for the UKCAT and the amount of time to spend on each section.

Determining How Long to Prepare for The Test

Exercise 3 - Determine how long to prepare for the test

Most students take the UKCAT at the end of the Summer, in either August or September. This is probably due to the fact that summer is a busy time. Many students will either be working or enjoying a break from their studies. Some students might be travelling, for part or all of the summer. Depending on your personal plans, there are any number of factors that could impact your decision on how long to prepare for the test. My advice would be to consider all the factors that might affect your preparation or performance on the test day and schedule your test appointment appropriately. Since you can choose any available test appointment, there is no reason not to choose the appointment that will give you the greatest advantage. Not taking into account other external factors that might influence preparation, I suggest determining how long you prepare for the exam based on how easy you find the official practice test in Step 2, if you found it ok then 3-4 weeks should be enough time to prepare. However, if you found it extremely difficult you may need longer. For those that struggle the most I personally think 6 - 8 weeks is more than enough time to prepare.

Recommended Preparation Time

Difficulty		Avgs Practice Score
Very Easy	2 weeks	> 700
Easy	3 weeks	650-699
OK	4 weeks	600 - 649
Hard	6 weeks	550 - 599
Very Hard	8 weeks	Below 550

Exercise 4 - Determine the Amount of Practice Time For Each Section

The strategy below helps give structure to preparation and provides a minimum number of hours candidates must commit to each section.

In order to calculate the recommended hours, follow these steps:

- Calculate the number of days till the big day (e.g. 30 days).
- Calculate the average number of hours per day you can realistically spend preparing for the exam (e.g. 3 hours per day, so that's 90 hours over 30 days).
- Dedicate 45% of the Total Time to your weakest section (e.g. 45% of 90 hours is 40.5 hours).
- Dedicate about 28% of the total time to the 2nd weakest section (e.g. 28% of 90 hours is 25 hours).
- Dedicate 18% of the total time to your 2nd strongest section (e.g. 18% of 90 hours is 16 hours).
- Dedicate 9% of the total time to your strongest section (9% of 90 hours is 8 hours).

This calculation is based on my personal experience and feedback from other high scoring candidates. Nonetheless, it should be used as a rule of thumb and act as a rough guide to help balance your time, you can modify or personalize as you see fit. I spent roughly 41 hours preparing for the Verbal Reasoning subtest and was able to improve my score significantly. By essentially spending 5 times more hours on my weakest section than my strongest section I saw a significant boost in overall score

Subtest	Strength	Priority	Minimum Time Allocated to Each Section
Verbal Reasoning	Weakest	1st	40.5 hours
Quantitative Reasoning	2nd Weakest	2nd	25 hours
Decision Analysis*	2nd Strongest	3rd	16 hours
Abstract Reasoning	Strongest	4th	8 hours

My priority table and the minimum time I allocated to each subtest

Once you've identified your true weakness and prioritised the UKCAT sections accordingly, the next part of my strategy is improving your skills, we will deep dive into techniques, tips and strategies to boost your score in each subtest.

Take a moment to breathe. When you're ready, let's get into Step Four and improve your skills.

Bonus Content

UKCAT Checklist - Key Things to Check Before Test Day

You only get one shot each year so don't rush into taking the UKCAT, it's an important part of your medical or dental application. Preparing for the test without an effective strategy will most likely result in achieving a low score

To help make sure you are preparing effectively this article covers some key questions to ask yourself before taking your UKCAT.

What is the minimum score I need?

This is the first question on the list, if you do not know the answer to this then it most likely means you haven't researched into your choices properly. You need to fully understand how universities use the UKCAT and use the information to set a target score. Without a target score for your practice tests and mocks, there is no way of knowing when you are ready to take UKCAT.

Which 4 Universities will I apply to if I achieve my target score?

Picking your final 4 choices is actually harder than what most students might think because medicine and dentistry are so competitive. You may need to be a bit more strategic, for example picking 2 of your ideal choices then maybe a couple other universities that do not rely heavily on the UKCAT. I recommend researching into all the schools that use the exam as well as the universities that do not require the UKCAT. Figure out how much emphasis all schools put on the UKCAT, this will help with making a more informed shortlist for your final.

Which 4 Universities will I apply to if I don't hit my target?

Hopefully you won't achieve below your target score. However, if you do, you may need to have a back-up plan. Have a shortlist of universities you'll consider if you score below your target score. However, do bear in mind your decile ranking as well, a score below target might still be in the top percentile and be fine if your choices do not have a cut-off. So do double check.

What are my weakest areas in the exam?

If you do not know your weakness in the UKCAT then you haven't taken enough time to assess your skills. To do well in the UKCAT you need to consistently improve your skill and assess your progress along way. The best way to identify your weakness is by attempting the official UKCAT practice tests without no prior preparation as this will identify where your natural capabilities lie. The results from this will help with identifying weak areas to work on.

What strategy and techniques can I adopt to improve my weakness?

Taking the UKCAT without an action plan for each subtest will not end well.

If you do not have a well detailed and laid out strategy for each section of the exam then you are not ready. How do you plan on saving on time on the verbal section? How do you plan on dealing with abstract questions you can't find the patterns for straightaway? How will you attempt difficult quantitative questions?

Step 4: Improve

Improving Your UKCAT Score

D espite what some candidates might believe, you can significantly improve your performance in the UKCAT. I'm living proof that you can, I went from scoring an average of 600 in each section to 710 by simply changing my approach to preparing for the exam. Like any other test you've taken in your life, the right preparation can significantly improve your test result. Instead of just practising questions, I focussed on improving my reasoning skills and perfecting a game plan for each section. In this chapter I cover each subtest and provide tactics, strategies and tips to improve your score in each one. Do not read this chapter in the order I've written it, start with your weakest section, take notes of the tips and exam strategies I recommend and put them into practice. Then move onto the next weakest subtest once you have become more comfortable. The more you practice these techniques, the better you'll get and the more confident you will be on the day of the test.

Tips, Techniques and Strategies for Verbal Reasoning

1. True, False and Can't Tell Paradigm

For some of the questions in the verbal reasoning section you'll be given a statement and asked to decide whether it's TRUE, FALSE or CAN'T TELL. To help tackle theses type of questions. Let's consider what each option mean:

TRUE means that the statement is correct based on the passage.

There are two main ways a statement can be true, firstly it can be directly stated in the passage. This is simple and easy to find in the passage. Let's consider the statement below:

KPMG has grown significantly since its launch in 1987. To date, a huge number of firms in the UK are using KPMG to run their auditing operations.

Statement: KPMG was founded in 1987

The statement is TRUE, as it is a direct match since it clearly states in the passage KPMG launched in 1987.

The second way a statement can be true is through inference from the passage. Based on the information the passage you can infer something is true, this is where the line can get blurred between True and Can't Tell. This is more difficult to answer, look at the statement below:

Statement: KPMG are a popular auditing firm in the United Kingdom

Even though the passage above doesn't directly say that KPMG are a popular auditing firm, you can infer from the passage that this is the case since a huge number of firms are using KPMG to run their auditing operations. This statement is True.

FALSE means that the statement contradicts the passage. Again, it may not be explicitly shown to be wrong, but instead you can detect it using inference.

There are two main ways a statement can be false. Firstly, through a contradiction, this is a direct mismatch where a statement goes against the passage factually or in terms of general opinion. The other way is when a statement goes too far, this is when it goes beyond the 'premise' of the passage. Let's consider the statement below:

Statement: KPMG is an investment management firm

The passage states that KPMG is an auditing firm, so the statement directly contradicts the passage. Therefore, it is False.

Statement: KPMG has slowed in growth recently.

The passage states that KPMG has grown significantly since its launch in 1987. The text alone does not give any indication how the firm is doing recently. However, the next sentence, starts with "To date..." which gives some indication on recent developments, so you can infer that KPMG is still growing. So, the statement is False.

CAN'T TELL means you cannot be certain based on the information provided in the passage. Consider the statement below:

Statement: KPMG is the best auditing firm in United Kingdom.

Even though the paragraph states that a huge number of firms in the UK are using KPMG, it will be too much of a leap to infer that KPMG is the best auditing firm in the UK. So, we Can't Tell as we do not have sufficient information.

Similar to the above examples, statements can be basic where they derive from a single keyword in the text and are essentially a direct quote from the text or easily validated by a single line or two of text. The above examples are very simple problems to help explain verbal concepts, and most, if not all, candidates should be able to answer these easily with a bit of practice.

In other cases, statements can be more difficult, based on insufficient information, that may require you to make inference or draw on multiple sources of text. Examiners tend to match keywords in the text, but contain information not found in the text. There are two main approaches used by examiners to trick candidates in the verbal section, they are as follows:

- **Broadening Scope:** This is where they take a statement or keyword from the text and then make it broader in scope than the passage. This is usually to confuse you to pick 'Can't Tell' instead of True or False. For example, the statement 'KPMG is the best auditing firm in the United Kingdom'.

- **Shift in Context**: This is where examiners might use qualifiers to make a subtle change of the context, sometimes by wrongly paraphrasing, to give a different twist or meaning to a statement. I'll cover qualifiers in more details later in this chapter, but it is vital to always look out for them.

By understanding the tricks used by examiners, you can reduce the likelihood of falling victim to them.

Another difficult type of verbal questions are multiple source questions, that require evidence from more than one area of the text and may rely on potentially more than one keyword when scanning the text for the answer. These questions tend to take longer to answer, and usually contain traps laid by examiners where candidates can mistakenly refer to only one piece of text and answer incorrectly. Keep an eye out for these as well.

To summarise,

A statement is True if the same information given in the statement is given explicitly in the passage.

In general, the statement summarises a complex piece of information in the passage by using paraphrasing and/or synonym words and terms.

Other time, the statement can take pieces of information that are spread out through different parts of the passage. Find these pieces of information quickly and verify each individual piece is true to confirm the whole statement to be true.

A statement is also True if you can correctly infer its content from the information. In this case, there must be enough information to make the inference.

It is important to rely SOLELY on the information introduced in the passage: Ignore your general knowledge and familiarity with the topic presented which might suggest that the information is invalid, you must use the passage alone as the source that can supply facts and information for making a decision. In other words, there is the possibility that the information in the passage will not be 100% correct.

Take note that your inference should not over generalise the details of the passage, even if it seems like a definitive answer. A seemingly correct answer presenting a broader inference than the one supported only by the information in the passage falls into the "Can't Tell" criteria.

A statement is False only if it directly contradicts something mentioned in the passage.

It is vital to double check the piece of information in the passage to ensure that it confirms the contradiction.

Some statements could be deliberately testing the accuracy of your reading comprehension skills and vocabulary. If you have any trouble with understanding a part of the passage, it is important to understand the broader context and verify whether the statement is correct or not in light of the whole passage.

Remember also that just because a statement is saying something different than the passage, this doesn't necessarily make it a false one. If it doesn't explicitly contradict the passage, it may still be a "Cannot Tell" answer.

Can't Tell means that the piece of information you are asked about is simply not given in the passage and that the passage gives no premise for correctly inferring the truth or falsity of the statement.

Contrary to some beliefs, this answer is the not necessarily the easiest to get right. In fact, it is often the hardest. True or False are often clearer to see; when the passage either explicitly states the same thing as the statement, then the answer is True, and when the passage clearly contradicts the statement, it is clear the answer is False. To determine that the answer is Can't Tell, you must ensure that the information needed to give a True or False answer is simply not available within the text. Ensure there is a clear basis for inferring something from the passage.

On other occasions, the statement could be a true or a false one according to personal knowledge. However, if the passage contradicts this or does not clearly imply it, then you must choose Can't Tell.

2. Comprehension Questions

These are standalone questions followed by four worded options that answer the statement. Examiners can include the beginning of a statement followed by four options of which one correctly completes the above statement. They include the following question-types:

- Incomplete Statements
- According to The Passage
- Except Question
- Most Likely

Unlike the True/False/Can't Tell questions, the statements must be True. Examiners include one correct option with three other False or Can't Tell options.

This makes these question-types sometimes harder especially for more complex passages.

So how do you attack comprehension questions? Here are 5 strategies to help improve accuracy and speed. Try each one and find the one that works for you, you can combine more than one approach, the goal is to discover what works for you:

Keyword Approach

The keyword strategy is one of the most popular techniques used by candidates where instead of reading the entire passage, you first read the statement or question:

Step 1: Read the statement

Step 2: Choose a keyword (or two) and scan the passage for the keyword.

Step 3: Carefully read sentence (or paragraph) keyword is located in the passage.

Step 4: Pick an option (or eliminate answers) based on findings.

A keyword can be a word, phrase or collection of multiple words, nouns (such as names, countries, places), dates and figures are great keywords because they can be easily found by scanning the text. It is important to scan for all the appearance of the keyword. If a keyword appears more than once you may have to combine information to determine the correct answer. There may be cases where you cannot find the keyword in the passage or you've found the keyword but no reference to the question, in this case the answer is almost always Can't Tell. I would recommend quickly looking again in case you've missed it or scan the passage again with an alternative method - either by picking a different keyword or looking out for synonyms (e.g. 'holiday' may be found as 'trip' or 'vacation').

It is important to note that scanning is not the same as reading, during scanning your level of comprehension is minimal. It is a shortcut to save time at the expense of comprehension, with enough practice you will get better at scanning. Once you find the keyword read the sentence or paragraph it appears to determine the correct response. If a sentence confuses you, reread it and the adjacent sentences if necessary, to try and fully absorb to information to the fullest extent.

The keyword approach is great for attacking True/False/Can't Tell questions, but I wouldn't recommend relying too heavily on it for comprehension type questions as you may waste time trying to prove each answer options and potentially get confused by irrelevant options.

Pseudo-Skimming

The Pseudo-skimming technique is a skimming technique where you only read the first sentence of each paragraph to get the main idea quickly. The first line in each paragraph usually introduces the topic being discussed in the paragraph so you can save time referring to specific paragraphs when answering individual statements instead of scanning the entire passage each time to answer a question. The general idea is that you put a little time upfront reading the passage but will save time overall answering the set of four questions related to the passage, because you will be able to quickly refer to relevant sections for each question.

Step 1: Read first sentence of each paragraph

Step 2: Memorise main idea.

Step 3: Read question then refer to relevant paragraph

Step 4: Pick an option (or eliminate answers) based on findings.

The passages in the UKCAT are usually two to four paragraphs long, this approach is great for passages that are 2-3 paragraphs long. However, for longer passages, you may need to combine pseudo-skimming with a mapping technique which we will discuss next.

Advanced pseudo-skimming involves reading the first and last sentences of each paragraph to get the main idea. Try and apply both levels of pseudo-skimming in order to see which one suits you best.

Passage Mapping

Passage mapping is a visual representation of the passage that shows the main idea surrounded by connected branches of associated topics split according to paragraphs or ideas. You will be given a laminated note board and a marker pen to draw your map during the test. Try pseudo-skimming (or scanning) each paragraph once. Use one word to describe each paragraph, trying to draw a mental "map" of the information and the logic in the passage:

Step 1: Pseudo-skim and scan each paragraph

Step 2: Draw a quick "map" of the information

Step 3: Read question then refer to map to answer it.

Step 5: For more complex questions, re-read sentence (or paragraph) topic is located in the passage.

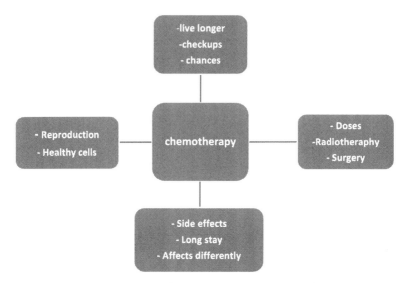

When drawing map only use keywords to save time. The passage map above is a quick map for a 300-word passage about the effects of Chemotherapy for treating cancer.

Aim to complete the map in 1 minute, that gives you 15 seconds to answer each question related to the passage. The idea is that you put a bit of time upfront to understand the passage so you should answer questions a lot quicker. During practice, time yourself to see how long this approach takes you and if it's suitable for you - with enough practice you should find this approach a lot easier.

'Keyword Diary' Technique

The Keyword Diary Technique is a great way to take the keyword approach to the next level. I came up with this technique the third time I took the UKCAT and it was a game changer for me. I realised the problem with the normal keyword approach is that you tend to waste a lot of time re-scanning the same text over and over again for each question.

Instead of looking for a specific keyword every time you refer to the passage, simultaneously keep an eye out for other keywords in the passage and write them down, these are other names, dates, places mentioned in the passage - split them according to the paragraphs where they are found in the passage.

Step 1: First count the number of paragraphs and jot on note-board as seen in image below (e.g. paragraph 1 is P1, Paragraph 2 is P2 and so on).

Step 2: Read the statement/question

Step 3: Scan the passage for the keyword in the question.

As you scan the passage for the target keyword, **simultaneously jot other potential keywords you come across in the passage** and allocate them to the paragraph they are found.

Step 4: Continue with Step 3 and Step 4 of the Keyword approach as normal.

You save time referring straight to your 'diary' instead of re-scanning and re-skimming the passage to spot a new keyword. Find below an example of a keyword diary for the passage about the effects of chemotherapy for treating cancer.

P1: Cancer, doses, radiotherapy
P2: Reproduction, blood, check ups
P3: effects, patients, life-cycle

Advanced keyword diary skills involve scanning the passage first and creating a keyword diary before attempting questions. Try and apply both levels of the dairy technique in order to see which one suits you best. This approach is great if you struggle to retain information of what you've read.

Elimination Technique

You will find yourself more than often in a situation where you have scanned the passage and found the relevant information but still stuck choosing the answer. No matter how difficult a statement, you can always eliminate one answer choice. For example, with True/False/Can't Tell questions:

If the statement is not supported by the passage, eliminate True.
If the statement does not contradict the passage. eliminate False.

For Comprehension questions:

Think about what you fully grasp from the relevant information in the passage then try mentally paraphrasing it in your own words into a simple sentence. At this point, make a quick judgement call and eliminate options that do not fit the same premise or may seem 'extreme' in context. Most of the time, you'll find yourself eliminating options that contradict what you know is definitely True or False.

3. Making Inferences - Read Between the Lines

We touched upon using inferences earlier in this chapter. To help with understanding this concept let's take a look at some other terms related to inference:

Logic is the science that evaluates arguments.

An **argument** is a group of statements including one or more premises and one and only one conclusion.

A **statement** is a sentence that is either true or false, such as "The cat is on the mat." Many sentences are not statements, such as "Close the door, please", "How old are you?"

A **premise** is a statement in an argument that provides reason or support for the conclusion. There can be <u>one</u> or <u>many </u>premises in a single argument.

A **conclusion** is a statement in an argument that indicates of what the arguer is trying to convince the reader/listener. What is the argument trying to prove? There can be <u>only one</u> conclusion in a single argument.

An inference is statement that is not directly stated in the passage but can be thought to be true based on the information in the passage. During the verbal reasoning test you will be required to make logical deductions from sentences, where you cannot infer too far and make a big assumption. For more difficult questions you may have to infer the main idea of the entire passage. To correctly answer some questions, a rule of thumb is not to bring your own understanding, knowledge or extra information into the text.

In many cases, an inference revolves around a set of 'premises' that have been established in the text that are used to reach a 'conclusion' not directly found in the text, but which is true based on those premises.

You can identify inference questions in the exam by the use of words such as conclude, conclusion, infer or inference in the question stem. Here are a few examples of inference questions:

Which of the following can be inferred from the passage?

Which of the following conclusions can be drawn from the passage?

According to the passage, which of the following must be true?

Another important point worth noting is that the correct answer choice is the one that makes <u>only a small step beyond the premises</u>. The inference is not a giant leap, and should not presuppose any assumptions, but rather be the immediate, closest conclusion that directly results from the premises. Moreover, the same tone (positive, negative, neutral) that comes across in the argument should also be present in the correct answer.

So how do you make inferences more accurately? Here are 2 strategies and techniques to help:

1. Deduction - Reach a simple logical conclusion

The concept of this strategy is **"If something is said in the passage, what is the logical extension?"** Deductions are very close to detailed statements, except that you must make a logical deduction, without using any knowledge besides what is provided in the passage. For example:

Amazon has become one of the most popular book retailers in the world, having a best-seller on the platform is becoming a dream for many established authors.

Statement: Amazon is the best book retailer in the world.

Is this statement a logical deduction based on the information provided in the passage? Perhaps, but it will be too much of a leap to infer it is the best book retailer in the world based on the opening statement "***Amazon has become one of the most popular book retailers in the world***". So the answer will be **Can't Tell**

Another form of deduction is where statements might involve some mathematics, this could involve simple mathematical operations, such as adding two or more numbers or comparing values assigned to specific subject matters. It is common for examiners to use numbers to side track candidates when, in reality, the statement is beyond the scope of the text and thus Can't tell. In terms of comparisons, two main types are usually seen in the exam. First is a simple comparison, asking essentially which value is larger. The second is more complicated and examiners can ask the same thing more indirectly, usually by comparing two dissimilar numbers (e.g. a percentage and a numeral). In that case, the numbers have to converted to the appropriate type to compare; otherwise, select Can't tell.

2. Paraphrasing - Answer in Your Own Words

This strategy cannot be applied to all comprehension questions, it involves answering the question in your own words before looking at the answer options to avoid getting confused by choices that may include irrelevant information.

This is great approach if you've invested some time upfront using the pseudo-skimming or mapping techniques to read bits of the passage beforehand. **If you can't come up with the answer in your own words before looking at the answer choices you run the risk of getting confused by options that include irrelevant information,** then waste time looking through the passage for information that doesn't exist.

4. Evaluating Extreme Language

Sometimes looking at the wording of a statement/question can help guide you to the correct answer. Statements can include **extreme phrases** (such as 'none', 'always', 'every time', 'must', 'definitely' etc) or **soft phrases** (such as 'might', 'may', 'could', 'sometimes', 'usually', 'often') that may shift the context of the statement.

Consider the statement "'Hair loss may be caused by stress" has a softer tone than 'Hair loss are caused by stress". The first statement uses a soft phrase (i.e. may) to suggest there is no doubt in the statement that hair loss can have another cause, or be a more complicated symptom, Thus the statement is True. However, the second statement uses an extreme tone in this case assumes that the evidence is conclusive, which is not the case and so this statement is either False.

In summary, if you see a soft phrase used in a statement it is likely the statement is True. If you see an extreme phrase used in a statement then it is more likely it is False or Can't Tell.

Soft Qualifiers: 'Might', 'Can', 'Sometimes', 'One of the (biggest)', 'Could', 'May', 'Usually', 'Often'.

Extreme Qualifiers: 'All', 'Every', 'None', 'Always', 'Never', 'Certainly', 'Impossible', 'Every time'.

In order for a statement with a soft qualifier to be False, it has to be **clearly stated** in the passage, and unless the passage makes it absolutely clear that an extreme qualifier is true, then it is most likely False.

A more difficult question in this category is one that moves the statement beyond the scope of the text and may require you to make an assumption, which in this case it's most likely Can't tell.

5. Passage Adjustments

Passage adjustment is a common trap laid by examiners, it involves slightly adjusting the statement to trick readers into picking the wrong answer. This is very common with True/False/Can't Tell verbal questions. Consider passage statement below:

> In 2010, FIFA officially announced that the 2018 world cup will be held in Russia.

Statement: FIFA announced the 2018 world cup will be held in Moscow.

The answer is Can't Tell. You might have been tricked and thought it was True. You can see that there is a slight adjustment here where the statement says Moscow. Even though, Moscow is the capital of Russia we cannot say definitely that the world cup will be held there so it is Can't Tell.

Obviously, it is easy to spot in the above small passage but in the exam, you might miss small details due to the longer text and time pressure. Examiners might also use **broader context** where the passage might refer to a specific situation but the statement may refer to the broader context or vice versa. Consider the excerpt below from a passage on the financial crash.

> 2008 saw the biggest housing market crash with over 35% of residential properties reclaimed by banks.

Statement: One-third of properties were reclaimed by banks

The answer is Can't Tell. The passage says one-third of residential properties were reclaimed by banks.

However, the statement is broad and does not specify which type of property, so it is not definite to assume that all properties were reclaimed by the banks. If the statement said 'one third of homes were reclaimed by the banks' then we could infer the answer would be True.

Once you have scanned the passage and found the keyword. Always read text carefully. A single word can change the entire meaning or context of the statement so keep an eye out for passage adjustment traps.

6. Writer Questions

Writer questions are verbal questions centred around the author's opinion or the opinion of others. In most passages in the UKCAT the author is anonymous. In essence, there is nothing different about this type of questions. They are often combined with other comprehension questions to add an extra layer of difficulty by making the author the focus rather than the text itself, when there isn't a real difference. Writer questions can cover anything from basic comprehension such as "According to the author…" to more unclear questions such as "What is tone of the author?" which requires a good understanding of the entire text. Inferences are required to answer broader type of writer questions such as "Which of the following is the author more likely to agree with?" or "The author most likely would not agree with: …".

How to Approach Writer Questions

Writer questions are time-consuming because they typically require deeper understanding of the passage, I would recommend attempting these questions with the pseudo-skimming or elimination techniques mentioned earlier.

Another form of pseudo-skimming commonly applied to this type of questions is reading the **first two lines and last two lines of the passage** to gauge the authors opinion before attempting questions. You may find it easier to read the question first then scan the passage for the correct answer then eliminating options accordingly.

If this is the case, also assess the options carefully and keep an eye out for qualifiers, if you see an option that uses an extreme qualifier it is most likely incorrect, answer options with good keywords and softer language tend to be right, so would recommend looking into them first. Also, you may see statements that seem unlikely based on common sense.

The opinion column in broadsheet newspapers like The Guardian and Daily Telegraph are a great starting point to work on your writer's question skills. Most opinion columns present logical arguments rather than neutral facts. This structure makes them ideal to analyse in the same way you would a verbal reasoning writers question. Try regularly reading an article then summarising the information. Keep shrinking down your summary until you've removed all the irrelevant fluff and meaningless words. You need to be able to summarise information quickly, if you can do this task quickly, you'll probably find the writers questions surprisingly easy.

7. Speed Reading Hacks

One of the main challenges in the UKCAT verbal reasoning subtest is timing. The idea that you can learn to speed read, that is, drastically improve your reading speed (with good recall and comprehension) has been around for quite a long time. We will briefly look in to the science behind reading and how you can realistically improve your reading speed before test day.

Reading is possible through eye movement but there are four different types of eye movement. For instance, there's something call smooth pursuit, which our eyes do when we are tracking a moving subject. There is also vergence when your eyes move closer together to focus on a subject in the middle of your field of vision.

There's also vestibular eye movement which is what happens when your eyes are fixed upon a fixed subject, but your head moves, and your eyes compensate for the head movement. But when we read our eyes move in quick jerky movements called saccades.

When we are reading silently to ourselves the average saccades length is about two visual degrees which equates to about eight letters on a page. This takes about 30 milliseconds to do. When your eyes stop and focuses on a text that's called fixation. To understand fixation, you need to understand the three ranges of vision your eyes have, the Foveal which spans about two visual degrees right in the centre of the retina, the Parafoveal which goes about five degrees on either side of any given fixation, and finally your Peripheral vision which is pretty blurry and can make out shapes and movement, but it can't pick up a whole lot of detail.

The foveal, by contrast, picks up detail very well and this is absolutely critical for reading. Most of what you can understand in any given fixation needs to be in that Foveal range. Maybe one or two letters can be in the Parafoveal range but that's it. The average fixation when your reading silently takes about 225 milliseconds, though it's an average. The range is typically anything from 100 milliseconds to 500 milliseconds. Furthermore, your reading speed isn't just determined by fixation and saccades. There is also the actual cognitive processing time that you have to go through in order to understand what you just read.

Now that you have somewhat of an understanding of the science behind reading, I want to share with you a few techniques that I learned to improve my speed reading.

1. PX Project

The PX project is a 20-minute exercise that has been scientifically proven to increase reading speed by up to 300%. The concept was introduced to me by Tim Ferriss, author of the 4-hour work week book.

As part of the exercise you identify you current reading speed then go through a number of exercises to track and improve within 20 minutes! With enough practice you can significantly improve your reading speed without compromising comprehension. For a step-by-step walkthrough the PX exercise, watch the YouTube video where Tim Explains:

WWW.YOUTUBE.COM/WATCH?V=ZWEQUW_YIJ0&T=1S

2. Finger Method

The finger method involves using your finger as a visual aid to read the passages during the exam. This reduces the likelihood of regression, back-skipping and the durations of fixations - therefore, increasing overall reading speed. Keep your eye fixated above the tip of your finger. It will serve as a tracker and a pacer to help maintain consistent speed and decrease fixation duration.

The UKCAT is computer-based so holding your finger against the screen might seem a bit weird at first. During practice, time yourself and compare how quickly it takes you to complete a passage with its accompanying 4 questions with this technique versus when you are not using it.

3. Reduce Subvocalization

Subvocalization is a very common habit amongst readers. It involves saying words in your head or out loud while reading and it's one of the main reasons why people read slowly and have trouble improving their reading speed.

Numerous studies have shown that eliminating this habit completely is not possible. Minimizing subvocalization will help you boost your reading speed, and it will also help you improve your comprehension. Reading isn't even about words, but rather about extracting ideas, absorbing information, and getting details.

Words by themselves don't mean much unless they're surrounded by other words. When you read the words "New York City", do you even think of it as three words? Most people would equate those three words (New York City) to a city. NYC would mean the same thing, right?

Many of the words we see are simply there for grammatical purposes (the, a, an). They don't provide you with the same kind of meaning as words like "university". We have to minimize subvocalization in order to boost our reading speed. Why do we have to do this? Because subvocalization limits how fast we can really read. Think about it this way: if you are saying each word in your head, doesn't that mean that you can only read as fast as you can talk? If you're saying every single word in your head, your limit is going to be your talking speed.

The average reading speed is about 150-250 words per minute (wpm). And the average talking speed is exactly the same. Because most people say words in their head while reading (subvocalization), they tend to read at around the same rate as they talk. You can test this out for yourself if you like. Try reading for one minute normally, and then try reading out loud for one minute. If you're like most people, your reading speed and talking speed will be similar (within 50 words higher or lower). If your reading speed exceeds your talking speed, that's a good thing to notice. We don't want to be limited to our talking speed.

Why do most people read between 150 and 250 wpm and not above 300 wpm? Because it's hard to talk that fast. Unless you do disclaimers at the end of commercials, it's difficult to talk over 300 words per minute. So subvocalization must be minimized because you don't want to get stuck reading as fast as you talk. You're capable of reading as fast as you can think.

Changing the habit of subvocalization is easier said than done. You can't just turn this voice in your head off. Instead of eliminating this habit, you want to minimize it. For example, let's say you're reading some text that said, "The boy jumped over the fence."

To minimize subvocalization, you might just say in your head, "Boy jumped fence," three words rather than six words in that sentence. Some people think this means skipping words, but you aren't actually skipping them. Your eyes still see all the words. You are simply just saying a few of the words. This is how you minimize subvocalization.

Keep in mind that there are a lot of words in sentences and paragraphs that are not essential to the meaning of that paragraph. We are reading for ideas, not words. Saying words in your head can sometimes be helpful. For example, when you are reading material that has technical terminology or vocabulary that you are not familiar. In situations like this, saying words in your head, or even out loud, can be a useful way to improve and expand your vocabulary. However, subvocalization can be useful. If you have to memorize something word for word, subvocalizing the words or saying the words out loud would be helpful. How do you think actors and actresses remember their lines? Reading out loud can help you memorize something word for word, but when you normally read, you very rarely need to know something word for word. Most of the time you are reading to extract information, ideas and details.

To boost your reading speed, you need to minimize subvocalization by **saying only a few words per line**. If you say every word, you'll be limited to your talking speed.

How do you know if this habit is changing? If you start reading over 300 words per minute, you are probably not saying every word in your head (because you can't talk that fast). If you are going over 400 words a minute, you are definitely making progress and probably just saying some of the words in your head.

3 Ways to Minimize Subvocalization

A. Use Your Finger to Guide Your Eyes While Reading

I keep on emphasizing the importance of using your finger to guide your eyes. It's a central principle to all speed-reading techniques and it's something that will help you minimize subvocalization. Using your hand to guide your eyes will also help you grab groups of words while reading, helping you avoid another common reading habit, fixation.

B. Practice Reading with Spreeder

Spreeder uses Rapid Serial Visual Presentation (RSVP) to help you boost your reading speed and minimize subvocalization. The application is simple to use. You simply paste the text you want to read into a textbox. Set your reading speed and press play. The words then blink on the screen at the speed that you set. You can also choose how many words you want to blink at a time. I recommend setting a speed of at least 300 words per minute. Any speed above 300 wpm will help you avoid subvocalizing all the words. The faster you go, the less words you will be able to say in your head. With some practice, you'll find it easier to minimize this habit of subvocalization.

WWW.SPREEDER.COM

C. Force Yourself to Read Faster Than You Normally Would

Let's say you normally read 250 wpm. Try going a little faster (maybe 300 or 350 wpm). If you force yourself to go a little faster than you normally read, you'll minimize the amount of words you say in your head. In addition to minimizing subvocalization, you'll also improve your focus because you have to pay more attention when you read a little faster. Again, the more you practice pushing yourself faster, the faster you will get.

8. Improve Retention

Retention is the ability to use short term memory to recall information you have just read to answer questions in the exam. There are many ways to improve retention during practice. We will look at three techniques that work well. I strongly recommend you give each one a try.

3 Ways to Improve Your Retention

A. Summary Technique

After skimming a paragraph, stop and take a quick second or so to summarize the main point to yourself of what you just read before moving to the next paragraph. This technique increases your ability to recall key points when answering statements especially for the comprehensive type questions where you may have to make inference.

B. Mc Gowell Grid

The Mc Gowell grid is a technique that involves capturing your personal reaction to the text in the passage. How you react is not particularly important but being able to reference part of the passage that made you happy, sad, in awe or angry, can be used to reference information about the topics in a passage.

C. Use the Elevate App

The Elevate app is a brain training application that uses cognitive games and exercises to improve focus, speaking abilities, processing speed, memory, math skills, and more. The app offers a rotating set of three games every day, each one targeted to specific brain functions like memory or math. You can pay to unlock more games if you're really into it, but you can keep practicing each of the three games as many times as you want each day until the set cycles out. It will also keep track of your progress each day so you can see how your scores match up, which can be helpful if you want to compare things like your performance in the morning to the afternoon on different days.

I would recommend playing their retention listening game to help improve your short-term memory for listening and comprehension. The more you practice the more difficult the exercise become and the better your retention becomes over time.

This skill can be applied to improving your retention for the verbal reasoning section, it will help with questions where you have to infer or combine information from two different sources in the passage.

WWW.ELEVATEAPP.COM

Tips, Techniques and Strategies for Quantitative Reasoning

In the pages to follow, I will share tips, techniques and strategies to help improve your error rate and reduce your chances of spending too long on numerical questions. After practicing the methods in this book for just a little while, your ability to work with numbers during the test will increase dramatically. With even more practice, you will be able to perform many calculations quicker. My goal is to teach you easy yet impressive techniques you can learn to do immediately for the UKCAT.

1. Scanning & Skimming Technique

Rather than reading and assimilating the entire data given in a question, scan or skim through question to understand the 'type' of data that you are given. Then, when you read the question, you will be able to determine quickly the relevant data you need to answer it. This approach will save you more time in the exam. With enough practice, you will be able to scan and draw out information very quickly under time pressure. Make sure to do the following during skimming:

- Focus on the relevant information – begin by narrowing down only the information you need, and then briefly skim through the data while ignoring the redundant details.

- Pay attention to the units – the question may refer to units than are different to those presented in the table/graph.

- Notice any additional information – such information can be provided in the headline, under the table/graph, or in an asterisk.

2. Visual Approximation - Inspection & Estimation

You will be surprised by the amount of questions in the test you can answer correctly by inspection, i.e. comparing data and answer options, without any calculations. This approach will save you a lot of time in the exam, I recommend try making logical deductions based on the data and options provided for questions that require one step calculations. A more accurate approach will be estimating data based on rounded figures.

Estimating is great to use when there a huge difference in the answer options or they are well spaced out. For example, if the answers are to the nearest thousands, and the data is given to the nearest ten, you can round the data to the nearest hundred. Another great time to estimate is to look for trigger words like 'approximate' or 'estimate' in the question.

In order to sharpen your estimation skills, try to practice solving several questions without performing the complete calculation and instead look for shortcuts and rely on estimations. Through practice, using these techniques will gradually become more and more natural.

3. Elimination

The art of eliminating is a vital skill that requires estimation and a bit of common sense. Ruling out answer choices that must be wrong based on rounded figures will help you move quickly through the section - does the option seem too big or too small? Where appropriate, start with the options and eliminate choices down to the two most likely answers and only calculating those options.

4. Basic Financial Concepts

I strongly recommend taking time solving problems on money such as costs, interest rates, profits, tax, revenues, stocks, inflation, etc. such as adding together the costs of a grocery list, dealing with percentage changes of profit, and calculating the price of a single ticket using simultaneous equations.

Questions can test the candidate's ability to deal with money in general. Questions can come with a verbal description and table of how tax is calculated, and the candidate is asked to find out how much tax will be deducted for a certain wage. The GCSE bitesize resource recommended earlier has some great tutorials and questions on these concepts. Play close attention during practice to sales (or cost) analysis questions, rates and trends as well as currency conversions.

5. Know Your Unit Conversions

Converting from one unit to another can help with answering some questions in the test. Examiners can try to catch you out sometimes so pay close attention to units when skimming data and question. Take some time to brush up on exercises until you are confident. For example:

1 km = 1000 m, 1 kg = 1000 g

1 m = 100 cm, 1l (litre) = 100 cl (centilitres)

1 m = 1000 mm, 1 g = 1000 mg (milligrams)

6. Snapshot of Answer Options

Before attempting each question, taking a quick look at the answer options can help with deciding how to tackle the questions. For example, if the answer options are close together in value you may be more suitable to work precisely to figure out the exact answer. However, if there is large difference between the options, it may be suitable to use estimation to pick the correct answer.

7. Learn Numerical Reasoning Shortcuts

One of the main challenges with the quantitative reasoning section is timing, there is a whole bunch of numerical shortcuts you can apply to help save time in the exam.

For example, say a question on speed, distance and time where the data was in Kilometres and hours (km/hr) but the question required you to calculate speed in metres per second. There are two ways to attempt this, you may try converting each unit to metres and seconds then use the required formula (distance/time) to derive answer. Second approach would be multiplying the distance in Km/hr with 5/18 to arrive at distance in metres per second - a quick shortcut.

There is a whole bunch of numerical shortcuts on the website maths-shortcut-tricks.com. I do not recommend learning every single one, instead during practice try to see what type of calculations take a lot of time to process in your head and see if you can find a shortcut for dealing with it. On the website you can find shortcuts and tricks for practically every type of numerical operation required in the UKCAT, from percentages, basic arithmetic, ratios and more.

WWW.MATH-SHORTCUT-TRICKS.COM

I particularly found tricks for calculating percentages, ratio and proportions helpful for the exam, check them out.

8. Minimise Use of Onscreen calculator

During the test you will be provided with on onscreen calculator. I strongly recommend to practise using it, however, be careful not to rely heavily on it. For instance, say you had a complicated question that required three steps of calculation to derive answer. I would recommend only using calculator for one of the three calculation steps. You lose time inputting numbers on the calculator, so limit its use during practice.

9. Flagging

Don't spend too much time on questions you cannot solve or may need a bit longer to calculate. Flag it and move on to the next question and keep your cool.

Where its taking long to figure out the answer, make logical deductions and flag it. If you have time at the end you can return and re-attempt questions.

10. Know Your Formulae

Several numerical concepts and formulae are required in the exam, having these at your fingertips so that you can apply quickly and accurately will help you perform to the best of your ability. Some of the most common formulae required in the exam include the following:

- Calculating averages
- Calculating speed, distance and time
- Proportions and ratios
- Percentages and percentage change
- Basic geometry - area, perimeter, circumference and volume of 3d shapes.

11. Mental Mathematics Tricks

Getting into the habit of calculating basic arithmetic in your head can save you valuable time in the exam - all it takes is a change in perspective. The quantitative reasoning is littered with these types of calculations. Usually, a given sum acts as one of several steps in your quest for the correct answer. The more you practice your mental arithmetic, the more time you will save.

Most of us are taught to do maths traditionally from right to left but if you want to do maths in your head (i.e. a lot faster) it's better to work from left to right. When you compute values from left to right it is easier process and estimate quickly.

The fundamental principle of mental mathematics - is to simplify your problem by breaking it down into smaller, more manageable parts. The numerical skills you require in the UKCAT will be for larger problems where a given sum acts as one of several steps to the correct answer.

There are many mental maths approaches for different operations, I urge to find the ones that are easy to grasp. To help I've provided below the key concepts you will need in the exam.

Addition

- Two-digit addition
- Three-digit addition
- Using complements (i.e. how far from number is from the nearest 100. e.g. 725 + 468 could be calculated quickly by '725 + (500 − 32)')

Subtraction

- Two-digit subtraction
- Three-digit subtraction
- Using complements (i.e. how far from number is from the nearest 100)

Multiplication

- 2 by 1 multiplication (e.g. 42 x 7)
- 3 by 1 multiplication (e.g 342 x 8)
- Rounding up approach (e.g 69 x 6 = '60 x 6' + '9 x 6')
- 2 by 2 multiplication (e.g 42 x 65)

Division

- One-digit division
- Two-digit division

Percentages

- Percentage of a whole number (e.g. 28% of 68)

Fractions

- Multiplying fractions

- Dividing fractions

- Simplifying fractions

Squares

- Squaring two-digit numbers

Rather than going through each operation one by one, during practice tests try to figure out which operation takes you the longest to calculate then learn mental tricks to save time. You can find the respective mental tricks on the blog.

WWW.THEUKCATBLOG.COM

12. Save Time with The Onscreen Calculator

A simple on-screen calculator will be made available for use during the test. it is a four-function calculator with the core **Memory** and **Num Lock** functions. I strongly advise familiarising yourself with the calculator during practice in order to save time.

Memory Functions (M+, M- and MRC)

The memory functionality is great for saving time in the exam. Let's take a look at each of the three memory functions:

Memory Plus (M+): Adds whatever is on the screen to memory register.

Memory Minus (M-): Subtracts whatever is on the screen from memory register.

Memory Recall (MRC): Recall the current memory register value.

The calculator is included within the practice questions on the official website you will need it for the next exercises:

WWW.UKCAT.AC.UK/UKCAT-TEST/UKCAT-PREPARATION/

Exercise 1: Solve the problem below using the UKCAT onscreen calculator

$$5 + 4 + 3$$

Steps:

- Press **m-** then **mrc**: This makes sure that your memory is clear (there is no need for this step if there is no m sign on the calculator screen).
- Now, press **5** and then **m+** (a small m usually appears on the screen to let you know there is something other than 0 in the memory) now press **mrc** (memory recall), you will see 5 (this is the current value in the memory).
- Now, press **4** and then **m+** (memory plus) now press **mrc** and you will see 9 (5+4=9).
- Press **3** and then **m+**, now press **mrc** and you will see 12 (5+4+3 = 12).

No matter what else you do on the calculator, as long you use no memory functions or switch off the calculator, that 12 will remain in the memory. The Memory function is useful when, for example, when you are doing a bunch of individual calculations and want to keep a running total of the sum of the results. See an example below:

Exercise 2: Solve the problem below using the memory functionality on UKCAT onscreen calculator

What is the total price spent for discounted item 1, item 2 and item 3.

Item 1: £100 at 10% discount

Item 2: £200 at 30% discount

Item 3: £150 at 20% discount

Steps:

- First make sure the memory is empty: Press **M-** then **MRC** (Memory = 0)
- Item 1 is £100 at a 10% discount: Press **100 * 0.9** = 90 **Press M+** (Memory = 90)
- Item 2 is £200 at a 30% discount: Press **200 * 0.7** = 140 **Press M+** (Memory = 230)
- Item 3 is £150 at a 20% discount: Press **150 * 0.8** = 120 **Press M+** (Memory = 350)

How much did I spend altogether? **Press MRC.** Screen will show 350!

To clear memory Press **M-** then **MRC** (the m sign on the screen will disappear)

You are aware that Pressing **M-** then **MRC** will clear the memory so it's important to be careful when doing subtractions using the **M-** function.

Exercise 3: Calculate the problem below using the UKCAT onscreen calculator

Calculate 5 + 4 - 3 using the memory function

Steps:

- Press **m-** then **mrc** (To clear the memory)
- Press 5 and then **m+**
- Press 4 and then **m+**
- Press 3 and then **m-**
- Press **mrc,** you would expect to see 6 (5+4-3 =6)

Unfortunately, 6 won't appear because you've cleared the memory pressing **m-** and **mrc** together at the end. They are two ways around this:

First Approach: Do the subtraction function in the middle of the calculation: i.e.

$$5 - 3 + 4 = 6$$

- Press 5 and then **m+**
- Press 3 and then **m-** (5-3=2)
- Press 4 and then **m+** now press **mrc** and would expect to see 6 (5-3+4 = 6).

Second Approach: Press ON/C button afterwards to clear screen

- Press 5 and then **m+**
- Press 4 and then **m+**
- Press 3 and then **m-**
- Press **ON/C** (the calculator screen will clear and show 0)
- Then press **mrc**, the number 6 should appear.

Percentage Functionality (%)

The percentage button is used to calculate any percentage of any amount.

Exercise 4: Use the UKCAT Calculator to solve the problem below

Calculate 22.5% of 1575

Steps:

This is a straightforward use of the percentage function, as follows:

- Type in **1575**
- Then press the **multiply** button (x)
- Type **22.5** then press **%** (screen will change to 0.225)
- Press **Equal** button (=) and would expect **354.375**

Let's try another one for practice.

Exercise 5:

Calculate 15% of 1674

Steps:

You would've typed in 1674, then press multiply (x), then press 15 followed by the percentage button then finally the equal button to give 251.1.

This is far quicker than using decimals. For example, you could have multiplied 0.15 by 1674 and arrive at the same answer. However, putting each digit in one by one takes longer.

Now try one on your own, using what you now know about the memory and percentage functions. Give the problem question another try.

What is the total price spent for discounted item 1, item 2 and item 3.

Item 1: £100 at 10% discount

Item 2: £200 at 30% discount

Item 3: £150 at 20% discount

How was it?

Steps:

- Make sure memory is empty: Press **M-** then **MRC**
- **input** 100 **multiply** 90 press **%** and = then Press **M+** (Item 1)
- **input** 200 **multiply** 70 press **%** and = then Press **M+** (Item 2)
- **input** 150 **multiply** 80 press **%** and = then Press **M+** (Item 3)
- Press **MRC** and you should expect 350

Make sure to use the calculator during your practice so that you can get acquainted with it before the test. Here are some tips to consider regarding the UKCAT calculator:

- Understand and use the different functions you can perform with the calculator so that you know what you can and can't do on it. It will save you time on the test.
- Getting familiar with the calculator will help you identify some of its common problems – this will help ensure you know how to input equations in the right order.

- Learn fast mental maths techniques to save time by reducing inputting equations for complex calculations.

- Practise will ensure you become familiar with the UKCAT calculator, resulting in quicker input of necessary information (numbers, functions, etc.).

The other functionalities such as square root and +/- are fairly straightforward, for that, I did not cover it in this guide, you can learn how to use the remaining functions on the blog:

WWW.UKCATBLOG.COM/

Tips, Techniques and Strategies for Abstract Reasoning

Despite what some may believe, you can improve your abstract reasoning capabilities in a reasonably short time. It has to do with efficiently learning a large number of typical, logical rules so that when you are faced with an abstract reasoning test question you will be able to quickly identify the relevant rule/s for this series of shapes.

The principles behind abstract reasoning questions has never changed. There are different patterns and logical rules that you will be required to apply throughout the UKCAT abstract reasoning test, and you'll need to do this in a timely manner. This is not something you can learn by only reading a book, but it is something you can quickly develop through a combination of practice and test-taking strategies.

1. S.C.A.N.S Method

S.C.A.N.S is a mnemonic to help structure your approach to the abstract reasoning questions. It serves as a useful basis upon which you can work out the rule governing patterns in a set. SCANS stands for the following:

S - Shape: What shapes are present?

C - Colour: What colour is each shape?

A - Angle or Arrangement: How are elements organised?

N - Number: How many shapes, sides, intersections, right angles etc?

S - Size or Symmetry: How does the size or symmetry of the elements vary?

By applying this list to each set, you can quickly spot commonality within each set, sometimes more than one rule applies, making some abstract questions more complicated. When trying to figure out relationships in a set work through each of the categories and begin to validate or reject relationships as you develop potential hypotheses.

2. S.P.O.N.C.S Method

S.P.O.N.C.S is another mnemonic for approaching abstract questions. It is pretty much the same as SCANS but in a different order, where colour is lower than the line for consideration. It also serves as a good basis upon which you can validate or reject simple obvious relationships for each set. SPONCS stands for the following:

S - Shape
P - Position
O - Orientation
N - Number
C - Colour
S - Size

SPONCS also includes another potential commonality - Orientation which refers to the position of an object relative to the box or other specified positions. For example, a set might have a specific shape always pointing up, or a set that has a triangle always pointing to a non-black shape in the box.

SCANS Vs SPONCS

In all honesty, it doesn't matter which mneonomic you use, just pick one that's easier to remember and practice adopting it during preparation. Most students find SCANS easier to remember, but it is really up to you.

Some of you may feel that pattern finding skills is a skill you cannot learn, but the truth is with sufficient practice, pattern finding can be learned and developed with an understanding of what kind of patterns to look for. The possibilities are endless with each category, so here are some key relationships to keep in mind when exploring each possibility:

Shape:

- Are all the elements the same type of shape (e.g. square, circle, etc)?
- Are the elements symmetrical or asymmetrical?
- Do the elements have curved or straight edges?
- Do the elements have right or acute angles?
- Is there an object which consistently appears in each box?
- Are shapes concave or convex?
- Are the shapes solid or dotted?

Colour:

- Are some elements always a particular colour?
- Does each box have a certain number of colours?
- Does the colour of elements influence the counting of some of the key features (e.g. black shapes have even number of sides; white shapes have odd number of sides)?

Position / Angle / Arrangement / Orientation:

- Does each element have certain shapes arranged relatively to each other?
- Does each box have rotated shapes?
- Does each box have elements arranged by features (colour, size, number of sides, etc)?

- Are some shapes always in the same place?
- Are some objects inside others?
- Do some objects point in a particular direction?
- Are some components arranged along the x-axis or y -axis (i.e. 'stand' vertically or 'lie down' horizontally)?
- Do shapes overlap or intersect?
- Are some shapes parallel or at tangent to each other?
- Do some shapes mirror each other?
- Does each box have an object pointing to a particular direction? (e.g. a triangle always pointing to a black box)

Number:

- Does each box have an odd or even number of shapes?
- Is the number of components or a particular shape the same in each box?
- Is the number of one type of shape the same?
- Is there a relative relationship between two different types of shapes (e.g. the number of black objects = number of white objects + 2)?
- Is the number of one type linked to a feature of another object (e.g. the number of dots in a box is equal to the number of sides of another object within the box)?
- Is the total number of edges of smaller shapes equal to the number of edges of the bigger shape (e.g. a box that has 2 small squares and 1 large octagon)?

Size:

- Are some objects the same size or are they all different sizes?
- Is a particular object small or big in each box?
- Is there a relative relationship between the shapes of two different objects? (e.g. When triangle is small the circle is big and vice versa)

3. The 'Simplest' Box Technique

This approach involves starting with the simplest box first when trying to find the pattern in a set. This is a good approach as the simplest boxes contain the fewest distractors, and thus will help you identify the true pattern. If the simplest box contains only one shape, your job becomes more straightforward. For example, if a box contains a single shaded circle in the corner of the box, you now have a clue that the pattern is either about circles, shaded shape or about arrangement in the corner. By checking other boxes in the set for these characteristics you will find the commonality quickly.

The simplest box technique can apply when looking at set A and set B. Most candidates instinctively start by looking for patterns in Set A, but if set B looks simpler then It's a better starting point. Once you've identified the pattern in Set B, you can then reverse the 'rules' for Set A and hopefully it will now be easier to spot.

4. Three-Square Rule

The three-square rule gives structure to the simplest box technique by comparing the two other boxes either side of the simplest box. The technique is as follows:

- Find the simplest box out of either set – normally the one with the fewest things inside it.
- Look at the two boxes either side of it
- Compare the three boxes, looking for any similarity with regards to the shapes, patterns, colouring or edges.
- Check if this works for the rest of the boxes in that set, and more importantly, not for any of the boxes in the other set.

If this works, Great! If it doesn't then repeat process again with the next simplest box.

The point of the three-square rule is to reduce the likelihood of confusion and create a reference point each time you validate or reject a hypothesis. It is helpful for very complex questions that may contain conditional patterns.

5. Avoid Matching

It can be tempting when you cannot figure out the pattern straight away to look at the test shape and find a similar looking box in a shape. This should be **avoided at all cost**. Always seek to find relationships in a set, you are better off finding partial relationships than matching boxes.

6. Never Start with The Test Shape

I strongly recommend to start looking at the patterns in each set before looking at the test shape. The test shape may not even have the pattern for either set, so you waste time if you start with it. Also, you run the risk of matching test shapes to a similar looking box in one of the sets. If you can't find a pattern straightaway, flag and move on to the next set of questions.

7. Beware of Conditional Patterns

Conditional patterns are where a characteristic of one object in a box dictates a characteristic of another item in the same box. This a popular scenario in difficult questions posed by examiners. For example, a pattern where each box contains a triangle and a circle, where if the circle is shaded it is positioned to the right of the triangle, if the circle is not shaded it is positioned to the left of the triangle. Conditional patterns are not that common so only really look for them if you can't find any relationships straightaway.

8. The 30 Seconds Mark & Flagging Technique

If you get stuck on a pattern for more than 30 seconds, FLAG and move on.

Most patterns you spot will jump out at you within the first 30 seconds, and it is much more important to answer each pattern than get stuck for 3 minutes trying to answer one of the more complicated ones. You may even be surprised how easily you spot the pattern when you come back to it, this is usually because by answering more questions your eyes become more trained.

9. Be Wary of Distractors

Distractors are shapes that have no relationships with other features in the box. You may find your yourself paying attention to certain elements that have no bearing on the relationship between objects. These tend to catch out candidates that overthink the entire pattern finding process. Just remember, if your hypothesis is correct, you will find no exceptions to the commonality rule within a set despite the difference between the elements in the boxes. Always remember this!

If a rule applies to a majority of the boxes in set but there is maybe one box that doesn't fit the rule, you've most likely fallen for a distractor. Recognise this immediately and switch hypothesis. There is likely something more complex going on like a conditional rule.

10. Focussed and Diffused Thinking

When trying to figure out patterns that do not come to you immediately try changing your perspective by moving closer and away from the screen. When you are close to the screen you are using focussed thinking, which takes advantage of your prefrontal cortex to focus on one specific set of data and concentrates on it, but it doesn't let the rest of your brain become activated. Thus, other patterns are more difficult to spot this way, a helpful trick is using diffused thinking where you move further away from the screen to change perspective.

Tips, Techniques and Strategies for Decision Making

1. Syllogism - Venn diagram Technique

Syllogisms can contain two or more statements that are followed by a number of conclusions. You have to use deductive reasoning to work out which conclusion follows from the information provided. For example, let's consider the statement and conclusions below:

Some Fishes are Vegan. All Vegans are Mammals

Place **'Yes'** if the conclusion follows. Place '**No**' if the conclusion does not follow:

- **All fishes are mammals.**
- **Some fishes are mammals**
- **Some vegans are mammals**
- **All the fishes are vegan**

You can choose to re-read the statement multiple times to work out which conclusions is valid or not. However, for some syllogism questions it may be possible to use Venn diagrams to visually depict the information. This technique creates a visual representation of the statement which can be easier and more convenient to deduce.

The statement above can be represented as the Venn diagram below:

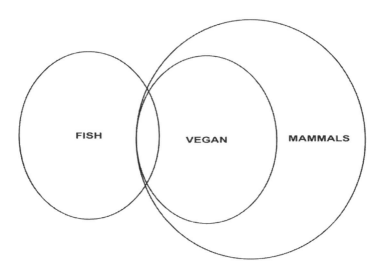

From the Venn diagram above we can see there is some overlap between Fish and vegan sets, and that the vegan set is fully enclosed in the mammals set. Now let's take another look at each conclusion:

All fishes are mammals: This is False because the Fish set is not fully enclosed in the mammals set.

Some fishes are mammals: This is True because some of the fish set overlaps with the mammals set.

Some vegans are mammals: This is False because all of the vegan set is enclosed in the mammals set.

All the fishes are vegan: This is False because the fish set is not enclosed in the vegan set.

I strongly recommend brushing up on Venn Diagrams beforehand, you find some helpful lessons on the BBC bitesize website.

Syllogisms in the UKCAT can be little more complex – there are five conclusions to assess based on each statement. Let's take a look at a more complex statement and apply the Venn technique:

Graduates that applied for jobs at Facebook were from either London or Kent. They either studied software programming or data analysis. Some of the graduates were from London and the rest studied data analysis

Place **'Yes'** if the conclusion follows. Place **'No'** if the conclusion does not follow:

- **All of the data analysis graduates were from Kent**
- **Some of the Kent graduates studied data analysis**
- **All of the software programming graduates were from London**

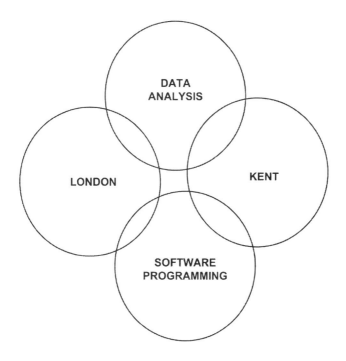

From the Venn diagram above we can see there is no overlap between London and Kent sets, and that both sets overlap with the data analysis and software engineering sets. Using the Venn diagram above let's attempt each conclusion:

All of the data analysis graduates were from Kent: False

Some of the Kent graduates studied data analysis: True

All of the software programming graduates were from London: False

In the exam, syllogism statements may be long and quite detailed or it may be short. With practice you'll soon be able to draw out key components in statements.

It's important to note that not every syllogism question can be solved using the Venn technique, but if appropriate I strongly recommend using it.

2. Syllogism - Pay Close Attention to Qualifiers

Qualifiers are words such as most, all, many, some, partly – that influence the context of the statement and thus influence the answers. These phrases are easily overlooked when read quickly. With enough practice you'll be able to spot them in any given text. The following are common qualifiers used in the exam:

'Most' refers to proportion, depending on the context may mean that it applies to an overwhelming majority.

'Many' refers to a large number but not necessarily the majority.

'Some' occurs often in the exam, refers to an unspecified amount, depending on the context could be a little or quite a lot.

'All' refers to proportion means 100%

3. Syllogism - Make Inference not Assumptions

Making an inference involves using what is explicitly mentioned in the statement to make a logical deduction about what is not. It is possible to make reasonable assumptions that are wrong if you use external knowledge and do not pay close attention to the text. A tip to reduce the likelihood of this happening is by looking out for qualifiers.

When picking an option reconfirm your choice by looking back to text or phrases in the statement. The qualifiers used in the sentence, the majority of the time, is the primary basis from which an inference can be made.

4. Syllogism - Apply Key Implications

Remember some of the Key implications you can make when attempting syllogism questions. They include the following:

All A are B also implies Some A are B and Some B are A

Some A are B also implies Some B are A

No A are B also implies No B are A

Using an earlier example:

Some Fishes are vegan. All vegans are mammals.

We can imply the following:

- Some Fish (A) are vegans (B) also implies some vegans (B) are fish (A).
- All vegans (A in 2nd sentence) are mammals (B in 2nd Sentence) implies some Mammal (B) are vegans (A).

5. Logical Puzzles - Table 'Fill-in' Method

Logical puzzles come in many forms in the Decision-Making subtest, they can be in the form of text, graphs or illustrations where you'll be asked to infer the information provided to solve the puzzle. The table method is a technique that can be applied when answering the most common puzzle format in the exam. Let's start by working through at a basic logical puzzle where the information is given in text where you have a number of clues from which to draw the best conclusion:

Four Rugby players (Matt, John, Jake and Paul) won 'Player of the month' at the Hackney Rugby Club in February, March, April and June. Each chose a retro designed coloured ball (from Red, Black, Orange and Green) as reward.

John won his award two months before Matt (who chode an Orange ball)

The Red ball was chosen first, the green one was chosen last

Which of the following statements must be **True:**
- **Jake chose the black ball**
- **Paul won his award In June**
- **The Black ball was won before the Orange one**
- **John won his award one month before Jake**

The question provides information and clues we need to pick the correct answer.
- **Step 1:** Take a quick second to think about what you need to know to solve the puzzle, in this case it is '**which <u>player</u> won which <u>colour trophy</u> in which <u>month</u>'**. By knowing the variables, you can draw a table to solve the problem. In the example above, the variables are: players, month and colour of trophy.

- **Step 2:** Organise the information by drawing a table. As a general rule, I recommend to start by including the sequential variable in the text, i.e. a variable that follows a logical order, in this example that would be the **Months** - Feb, March, April and June along the first column as seen in the table below.

Month	Players	Colour Rugby Ball
Feb		
March		
April		

June		

- **Step 3:** Look at the clues provided. The text includes two clue, in the exam, expect the clues to be standalone sentences from the main passage as illustrated in the example.

First Clue - *John won his award two months before Matt (who chose orange)*

First thing you notice is the straightforward clue that Matt chose orange. You will fill this into your table. Did you notice that the months given are not consecutive? This helps a bit. Therefore, John must have won his award in either February (two months before April) or April (two months before June) and that Matt must come in April or June.

Month	Players	Colour Rugby Ball
Feb	John (?)	
March	John (?)	
April	Matt (?)	Orange(?)
June	Matt (?)	Orange(?)

(?) refers to may be a possibility

Second Clue - *The red rugby ball was chosen first, the green one was chosen last.*

Since the green rugby ball was chosen last, revisiting the first clue - The Orange cupcake must have been chosen – by Matt – in April and therefore John must have won his award in February (i.e. first award chosen - Red ball).

Month	Players	Colour Rugby Ball
Feb	John	Red

March		
April	Matt	Orange
June		Green

We can fill in our table a bit more, since there are only 4 colour balls we can deduce that the Black ball must have been awarded in March.

Month	Players	Colour Rugby Ball
Feb	John	Red
March	Jake or Paul	Black
April	Matt	Orange
June	Jake or Paul	Green

You don't need to complete the table to get the correct answer. In fact – most times the data is arranged so you can't complete the table.

Let's take another look at each answer option:

Jake chose the black ball

Looking at the table this is possible but it may not be true either. It is also possible that Paul chose the black ball.

Paul won his award In June

This is possible but it may not be true either. It is also possible that Jake chose the black ball.

The Black ball was won before the Orange one

This MUST be True so it is the right answer

John won his award one month before Jake

Again, looking at the table – this may be true but it also may not be.

In the exam, use short codes to save time when drawing your table, as seen in the table below:

Mo	P	C
Feb	Jo	R
Mar	Ja or P	B
Apr	M	O
June	Ja or P	G

I strongly recommend during practice to pay attention to your speed in drawing out tables and answering logical puzzles. **Also, note that you do not need to complete the table - just fill in sufficient information to answer the question.**

6. Logical Puzzles - The Cross-Hatch Grid Method

The Cross-Hatch Grid Method involves using a grid-like approach to solve logical puzzles. It works very well for questions where you have three non-sequential variables. Let's take at another example and solve it using the Cross-Hatch Grid method:

Monica, Joanna, Maria and Patricia work for Net-a-porter. Their company cars are different colours: Red, Yellow, Green and Blue. As

it happens, each lady drives a different type pf car: Ford, Toyota, Peugeot and Honda.

Monica has a Yellow car

Joanna has a Peugeot and Patricia has the Honda

The Ford car is blue

Which of the following statements is must be **True**?

- **Monica has a Ford**
- **Patricia has a yellow car**
- **Joana did not have a blue car**
- **Patricia has a Red car**

The question provides information and clues we need to pick the correct answer.

Step 1: Take a quick second to identify and number the variables in the question.

They are three variables and they include employee **Names** (Monica, Joana, Maria, Patricia), car **Colour** (Red, Yellow, Green, Blue) and car **Type** (Ford, Toyota, Peugeot, Honda).

Variable 1 - Names

Variable 2 - Colour

Variable 3 - Car Type

Step 2: Once you have identified your variables construct your Grid.

It can seem daunting if you've never constructed one before, but don't get discouraged - once you learn a few basic rules you'll be on your way to constructing grids very easily and quickly.

In order to construct your Grid, you need to first know the variables and number of items within each one. Every logical puzzle in the exam has a set number of variables (usually three or less). In this example there are THREE - Names, Colour and Type. Also note that each variable has **four items** (e.g. Colour has Red, Yellow, Green and Blue).

Every item is labelled on either the left-side or the top-side, or both sides of the grid, depending on the variable it is in as seen below:

The larger areas where each variable intersects are called sub-grids. Each sub-grid is always a square that is outlined in a slightly heavier black line. There are three sub grids in the above cross hatch grid (i.e. Top left, Top Right and Bottom Left).

The overall grid is a weird shape, it looks like a piece from the game Tetris. To help you with the structure of your grid you will use the formulae:

Number of Sub-Grids in first Column = N - 1

Where **N** is the total number of variables.

The number of sub grids in the first column is equal to the number of variables (N) minus one. The second column would be N minus two and so on. In the example there are three variables if we used the formulae to work out the number of sub grids in the third column we will arrive at zero. So the grid stops at the second column, where the first column has 2 sub grids and the second has only one. When constructing a grid always start from the top, as you can see in the grid shown that the second column has the sub grid at the top not bottom.

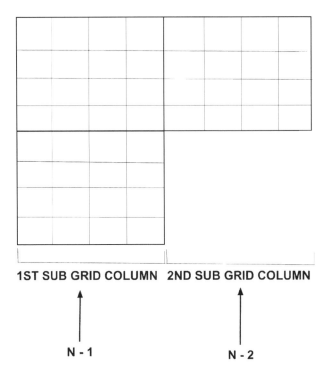

1ST SUB GRID COLUMN   2ND SUB GRID COLUMN

N - 1   **N - 2**

The next part of constructing the grid is including the variables and items, in the example problem, there are three variables with four items each.

Key Rules for Drawing A Grid

General Rule: You would have noticed that there is a set number of variables that you can place on the grid due to the N -1 rule. For instance, a three variable grid will include 2 variables along both sides of the grid. Whilst a four variable problem you will include three variables along both sides, a five variable problem you will include four variables along both sides and so on.

Since the example has three variables we have included two variables on both sides. The left side has the **Names** and **Colour** and the Top side has **Type** and **Colour**.

TOP SIDE

Left Side Rule: For a three-variable problem, always place Variable 1 at the top sub grid and Variable 2 at the bottom sub grid. You can apply this to problems with more variables, for instance if you had a four variable problem you would have three sub grids in the first column (using N -1) so the Left side will include Variable 1 at the top, second sub grid below that would be variable 2 and the bottom sub grid will be variable 3.

Top-Side Rule: Always start with the last variable then work backwards as you move from left to right of the grid, in other words, the first sub grid column would be the last variable, the second sub grid column would be the second to last and so on.

For example, with a 4 variable problem the first sub grid column will have Variable 4, the second sub grid column will have variable 3, the third column will have Variable 2 and so on.

In our example, Variable 3 is **Type** and variable 2 is **Colour** so these will be placed in the top side as seen above.

Once the variables are correctly placed fill in the grid with the items:

	Ford	Toyota	Peugeot	Honda	Red	Yellow	Green	Blue
Monica								
Joana								
Maria								
Patricia								
Red								
Yellow								
Green								
Blue								

Every item on the grid has a column and/or row representing it. Each column and row travels across the full width and height of the grid at point (height and widths will vary depending on the number of variables).

Step 3: Look at the clues and fill in the grid.

We will fill in the grid using ticks (√) and crosses (x) at the intersections where items meet. The example includes four clues:

Clue 1 - *Monica has a Yellow Car*

We will put a tick in the box that intersects Monica and Yellow.

Clue 2 - *Joana has a Peugeot and Patricia has the Honda*

We will put a tick in the box that intersects with Joana and Peugeot, another tick at the intersection of Patricia and Honda

Clue 3 - *The Ford car is Blue*

We will put a tick in the box that intersects Ford and Blue.

Clue 4 - *The Honda car is not Red*

We will put a Cross (X) in the box that intersects Honda and Red.

	Ford	Toyota	Peugeot	Honda	Red	Yellow	Green	Blue
Monica						✓		
Joana			✓					
Maria								
Patricia				✓				
Red				X				
Yellow								
Green								
Blue	✓							

Step 4: Add Cross (X) to the Grid where it can be inferred.

There are two rules to remember when filling in the cross grid:

❶ Every item in a variable is matched to only one other item in another variable. For example, each car type has only one colour.

❷ No two items in the same variable will ever be matched to the same item in another variable. For example, Monica and Joanna cannot both have the same car.

Following this logic, you can add additional crosses (X) to the grid **along the same rows and columns where you've drawn a tick BUT it must be within the same sub-grid**.

	Ford	Toyota	Peugeot	Honda	Red	Yellow	Green	Blue
Monica			X	X	X	✓	X	X
Joana	X	X	✓	X		X		
Maria			X	X		X		
Patricia	X	X	X	✓		X		
Red	X			X				
Yellow	X							
Green	X							
Blue	✓	X	X	X				

If we explore this further, it makes sense when you think about it. Since Monica's car is Yellow, we can infer that other colours are invalid and that other names (i.e. Joanna. Maria and Patricia) do not have a yellow car.

With enough practice you won't even need to do this step you'll be able to visualise it mentally. To save time in the exam, only use this step for difficult questions where you cannot spot the answer after Step 3. In fact – all of the time the data is arranged so you can't complete the grid so don't dwell on completing it, **stop at the point where you can validate or disprove each answer option**.

Step 5: Eliminate Answer options and Solve Problem
Most of the time if not all, you don't need to complete the grid to get the correct answer. Let's look at answer options provided in the exam.

Monica has a Ford

Since Monica has a Yellow Car and The Ford is Blue. This statement is False.

Patricia has a yellow car

Since Monica has a Yellow Car, therefore Patricia cannot have the Yellow car. This statement is False.

Joana did not have a blue car

Since Joanna has the Peugeot and the Ford is the Blue car. This Statement is True.

Patricia has a Red car

Since Patricia has the Honda and the Honda is not Red - This statement is False.

Fill-in Method Vs Cross Hatch Grid

It is difficult to know when to use either methods when solving a logical puzzle. Most of the time you can't tell which kind will work best until you've spent a lot of time trying to solve the puzzle with the wrong kind. Generally, I found the fill-in method works better when you have at least one sequential variable that follows a logical order, for example months of the year, days of the week or numbers.

The Cross-hatch grid works better when all your variables are non-sequential, for example names, colours, star signs, etc) i.e. variables that do not follow any logical order.

I strongly recommend during preparation to practice both methods when attempting questions in order to train the brain. However, do not rely too heavily on them in the live test as they can be time consuming.

The reason why I shared these methods with you is to help you develop the mindset for dealing with logical questions, **always use shortcuts wherever possible to answer the questions**.

Aim to get to a point where you don't need to construct an entire table or grid to arrive at the answer - Elimination is a great strategy where you interchange between reading the question as well as the options before arriving at the answers.

As you get more comfortable with logical puzzles, Practice skipping steps and using shortcuts wherever possible when constructing table or grid, practice evaluating and eliminating options while filling in the table or grid.

7. Practice Interpreting Graphical Problems

Solving graphical problems is what you can expect in the quantitative reasoning subtest. However, in Decision Making expect to interpret graphical data. You can be provided data in the form of any of the following:

- ✓ Tables
- ✓ Bar charts or Histograms
- ✓ Scatter Plots
- ✓ Pie charts
- ✓ Line graphs
- ✓ Schematic
- ✓ Venn Diagram

Then be required to interpret the information and draw conclusions, by placing a 'yes' or 'no' answer next to the conclusions provided. The best way to improve this skill is by solving as many graphical problems as possible before test day and getting into the habit of analysing the data first. Instead of jumping into the question and then going back to the data to look for an answer. Read all of the labels on the presented graph or table. What is in each column? What is in each row? What is the range of values? Does the data have a direct or indirect relationship? Do the lines have positive or negative slopes? Where was there the most change or growth? Where was there the least? With this kind of discipline, you will already understand what is being presented. The question becomes almost an afterthought, and you'll know exactly where to look for the correct information.

8. Practice Interpreting Venn Diagrams & Solving Venn Problems

The Decision-Making subtest is sprinkled with a lot of Venn problems that come in many different forms. The most common form are as follows:

- **Text to Venn:** This is when a question gives information in text and answer options are in Venn diagrams, and you are to choose which of the answer options fits the information best. There are also problems that do not ask you to draw a Venn but drawing one will help solve the problem.

- **Euler Diagrams:** This is when you are given a list of items in sets and be asked to choose the correct Venn diagram to represent the group of items.

The best way to improve your Venn skills is with practice. I would recommend spending an entire day on just Venn practice, there are so many questions that require Venn knowledge in the Decision-making subtest. So make sure you fully grasp key concepts and are comfortable solving Venn problems before your big day. I would also recommend practice range of problems that are within the scope of the exam so that you are fully prepared for whatever puzzle the exam throws at you.

9. Practice Solving & Interpreting Probability Problems

Probability is another key concept to understand for the Decision-Making subtest. In the exam, probability questions can come in many forms. You will be presented with a passage with statistical information and be asked to select the best possible answer. The best way to prepare for this is to practice as a many probability questions within the scope of the exam. Practice the elimination technique and make sure to read question/options carefully.

10. Elimination Technique - Interchange & Re-Read

We have touched upon elimination earlier, this is where you eliminate answer options one-by-one until you arrive at the correct one. Interchange between reading the question as well as the conclusions before arriving at the answers. Always evaluate each and every conclusion before selecting answer.

Questions where you have to evaluate arguments, for or against, a particular solution for a problem - make sure to select strong arguments that are directly connected to the subject matter. Weak arguments rely on opinion or assumptions. **As a general rule, eliminate statements that are assumption**s.

Situational Judgement

The situational Judgement is the final subtest of the UKCAT. Unlike the other subtests, you do not receive a scaled score from 300 to 900. Instead, you are assessed from Band 1 to Band 4. The bands reflect the degree to which the answers you choose match the answers chosen by a panel of medical experts; Band 1 means that most of your answers were the same as the panel of medical experts, Band 4 means that very few of your answers were the same. Thus, your aim in the situational judgement is to pick the same answer as the panel. You have 26 minutes to answer 68 items, that is 19 scenarios, each accompanied by 2 to 5 items. The scenarios are drawn from real-life medical and educational situations, and you must consider how a doctor or dentist, or medical student would respond in the circumstance described.

Situational Judgement - Question Types

The Situational Judgement questions do not require any medical or procedural knowledge – There are two types of questions in the test, they include:

Appropriateness Questions: This part of the test account for roughly 60% of the items. This is where you are given a scenario and presented with an action. You will then need to rate how appropriate this action is in the context of the scenario. You are then given four answer choices to choose from, they include:

- **a very appropriate thing to do** – if it will address at least one aspect (not necessarily all aspects) of the situation.
- **appropriate, but not ideal** – if it could be done, but is not necessarily a very good thing to do.
- **inappropriate, but not awful** – if it should not really be done but would not be terrible.
- **a very inappropriate thing to do** – if it should definitely not be done and would make the situation worse

Importance Questions: This accounts for approximately 40% of the items. This is where after each scenario you are presented with an action. You need to rate how important it is to carry out that action in the context of the scenario. Those actions which are considered essential should be awarded high importance. If an action is inconsequential, or even detrimental, then if will be of lower importance, you are then given four answer choices to choose from, they include:

❶ **very important** – if this is something that is vital to take into account.

❶ **important** – if this is something that is important but not vital to take into account

❶ **of minor importance** – if this is something that could be taken into account, but it does not matter if it is considered or not.

❶ **not important** – at all if this is something that should definitely not be taken into account

Tips, Techniques and Tactics for Situational Judgement

1. Understand the Conflicting Issue

There is always the temptation to quickly scan the text before answering a question. I would strongly recommend not rushing, always read the scenario properly before attempting the question, as you must understand the conflicting issue involved before deciding on appropriateness or importance.

2. Approaching Scenarios

Always answer questions based on how one **should** act in a professional setting rather than how they may likely act. Never answer questions based on how you would personally react. For medical or dental settings, think using the key principles of good medical practice and respond accordingly.

3. Treat Response Options Independently

Always treat response options independently - you should make a judgement on the appropriateness or importance of an option independent of the other options presented within the scenario. Make sure to answer within the perspective of the character identified within the question.

4. Know Your Character

The first thing you need to pay attention to in every scenario is the character or profession of the person involved (e.g. junior doctor, consultant, nurse etc). This is particularly important for when looking at the duties of a medical student compared to a fully trained doctors.

Even though both must display the same competencies, generally medical students might not be as knowledgeable, so depending on the scenario you might have to take that into account that reporting to a higher authority might be appropriate/ important. Typically, scenarios that compromise patient safety, confidentiality and data handling must be reported to higher authority.

5. Be Aware That Not All Possible Responses Will Be Provided

The response options provided in the situational judgement are not meant to represent all possible responses. The response you think may be most appropriate may not be included in the options. Some options may be appropriate or important in the short term, while others may be appropriate or important in the long term. Consider options relevant of the timeframes, because an option may be an appropriate thing to do even though it might not be done immediately.

6. Browse the GMC Documents

The *Good Medical Practice* and *tomorrows doctors* are great blueprints that gives detailed advice on how doctors should behave. Many of the principles and themes of the situational judgement test are derived from this document so I strongly recommend reading them beforehand.

7. Review Official Test & Practice Questions

At some point during preparation review the scenarios provided in the official practice questions and test, try to understand the conflicting issues in each question and refer, when necessary, to the GMC good medical practice guide to help with picking the correct response. Understand answers to each item and take notes of key principles that you may need to brush up on. The goal here is to gain familiarity with the key principles of the test.

8. Practice Making Snap Judgement

Once you have got more comfortable with the key principles of medical professionalism and have spent plenty of time improving your error rate. Start to work on speed, get used to making snap judgment and choosing a response option quickly and confidently as possible. Whilst there will be questions that are tough to assess, a majority of the questions are relatively straightforward and you will save valuable time picking quickly.

9. Do Not Overthink! You Can Still Get Half Marks

Try not to get too caught up in what the 'right' answer. Situational judgement questions are really easy to overthink if you dwell on them too long, because you could always make an argument that something is more or less appropriate based on other factors. Take the sentence that you're given and go with what you know to be true based on it. Remember that you get half marks for being on the right 'side' (appropriate/inappropriate).

BONUS EXERCISE!

Have a question regarding preparation?

Ask a question in THE UKCAT BLOG private Facebook study group. The group boasts hundreds of students taking the exam. I'm sure you'll get your questions answered there.

Access details to the private Facebook group are included in the companion course so make sure to subscribe to it!

I look forward to seeing you in the group!

Step 5: Practice

Practising UKCAT Questions

Most candidates skip the earlier steps and dive straight into practice. This leaves them at risk of only familiarizing themselves with the exam and not improving their reasoning skills. In extreme cases, some candidates may spend a majority of time practising subtests that they are more comfortable with and subconsciously neglect more difficult ones. This creates a false sense of assurance which is eventually shattered when they take a mock test or worse, the real test. To avoid falling victim to this, I encourage you to go through the earlier stages in this book before doing this step.

Once you have identified your weakest subtests and have a handful of techniques you would like to give a go, come back to this section to learn how to put them into practice. We will have a look at the sub-strategy for practising questions and later dive into study hacks to boost productivity during revision.

The goal is to ultimately ensure you work hard and smart, let's take a quick look at the general overview of the practice sub-strategy:

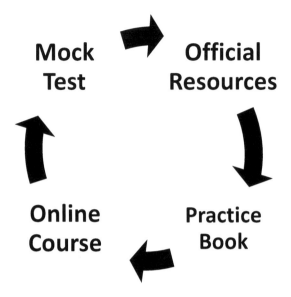

Work on one subtest at a time, starting with your weakest subtest go through each stage of the sub-strategy above then move onto your next weakest subtest and repeat. The idea is that you focus on one subtest at a time starting with your weakest one.

Each stage in the practice strategy focuses on the type of resource to use, we will now discuss how to practice questions at each stage and what key performance indicators (KPIs) you need to pay attention to during practice.

Official UKCAT Resources

We used the official practice questions and tests in Step 2 to identify your weaknesses in the exam, and you probably reviewed answer rationales upon completion which is good. Once sufficient time has passed, usually three to five days, revisit the practice questions and test for the UKCAT section you would like the to practice. For instance, if you are focusing on verbal reasoning only go through the verbal question bank and the verbal section in each practice test.

You want to attempt the questions untimed at your own pace and learn from the answer rationales of questions again, but this time use the tips, techniques and tactics provided in Step 4 when applicable as you attempt questions. However, be sure to keep a close eye on the following KPIs:

Error Rate: The frequency of questions answered incorrectly when attempting questions in a specific subtest. It is calculated as a percentage, the more questions you get wrong the higher the value. For example, if you get 10 questions wrong attempting 44 verbal questions then you have a verbal error rate of 22%.

Question Type Analysis: An analysis of your performance with respect to the question-type in each subtest. For example, which question-type in the verbal section is most difficult? Which one is the easiest?

Game Plan Evaluation: An evaluation of how well the tips, techniques and strategies work. The idea is that by the end of your revision you will have a shortlist of techniques you will use on test day. For instance, how well does the keyword strategy work for you? Does pseudo-skimming improve your comprehension?

Environment Analysis: An analysis on how comfortable you are with computer-based tests. Since the official practice questions are in the same format as the exam, it's important to pay attention to how you find working in a computer-based environment.

These KPIs are designed to help evaluate your progress as you attempt the official practice materials, we discuss them at great depth in the next chapter. For now, pay attention to the above KPIs as you attempt the official questions and take note of your findings.

Try to find ways to improve your performance, try thinking out of the box, is there a technique you can adopt to improve your error rate? Is there a resource online you can use to gain more familiarity with a specific question type? Do you need to adjust your exam technique? Do you need to practice more questions using a computer to be comfortable with the testing conditions? These are some of the key questions I encourage you to ask yourself as you use the official practice materials. Depending on the outcome of your practice, you may want to work on improving each KPI before moving onto the next stage using practice books.

UKCAT Practice Book

Practice books are great resources to prepare for the exam, with the best-selling practice books boasting of thousands of questions that replicate the breadth and depth of the different types of questions that can be asked in the UKCAT. Even though these resources are great for familiarising yourself with the exam, practising questions does not mimic the testing environment that you will expect in the UKCAT. For this reason, I propose using these books to just gain more familiarity with the questions in the exam, learn more tips and strategies for dealing with each subtest rather than focusing on speed or timing. I would even recommend attempting the mock exams provided in these books at your own pace, do not time yourself. The idea is to get you more familiar with the exam and improve your error rate, place more emphasis on honing the test strategies you've learned. However, keep track of the following KPIs:

Error rate: Monitor your error rate in each section as you practice questions in the book. Make sure to know your error rate for each section as we will refer back to this later, put into practice tips, techniques and strategies learned to improve this.

Question-type analysis: Rank the questions-types in each subtest based on level of difficulty, spend more time working on the most difficult question-type, once comfortable move to the next type of questions. This may require you to explore other resources online or use old text books to improve.

Mock subtest Analysis (untimed): Some practice books have mock exams included, I recommend not to attempt them in order, start with your weakest subtest - use the conversion table on the blog to work out your score out of 900. You may choose to time yourself if you want but I strongly recommend to emphasis on improving your error rate at this point.

Game Plan Re-Evaluation: Re-evaluate the strategies and techniques you are using. Which ones are working? Which ones aren't? The idea is that you hone the strategies that work and stop or adjust the ones that aren't working so well.

Since books do not replicate the testing environment there is no point doing environment analysis or monitoring your speed.

I must also mention that you shouldn't read UKCAT books cover for cover, start with the chapter of your weakest section and go from there. I remember the first time I took the UKCAT I bought like three of the best-selling books at the time and read them cover for cover, guess what? my UKCAT preparation was hindered. Thus, the mediocre score.

BONUS TIP

Advice on Picking A UKCAT Practice Book

UKCAT books are great when preparing for the exam. They provide practice questions and helpful tips to help students familiarise themselves with the UKCAT.

Even though they are not official UKCAT resources, studies conducted by the UKCAT exam board suggest that use of practice books significantly improves a candidate's overall score. Unfortunately, there is a long list of practice books available, so how do you go about picking the right one for you?

The following are **KEY** factors to consider when picking a UKCAT practice book:

#1. Number of Practice Questions

The total number of practice questions included in a book is important. Obviously, the more practice questions the better. The best-selling books do their best to replicate the breadth and depth of the different types of questions that can be asked in the exam and cover the spectrum of difficulties as well. However, make sure to also take into account the ratio of practice questions. If you find the verbal reasoning section the hardest of the five subtests, it may be smart to get a practice book that contains a higher ratio of verbal questions so that you can practice more and improve your overall verbal skill. You can usually find this information in the book description.

#2. Number of Mock Exams

Mock exams are a great way to further identify any area of improvement in time management and dealing with pressure. They also help give you an indication of what you a likely to score in the live tests. I recommend attempting at least 3 mock exams before test day. The more mock exams a book provides the better you'll be able to gauge how you manage time our and handle the pressures of the exam.

#3. Detailed Explanations, Tips & Techniques

You will find yourself referring to answer rationales for items you find difficult. In-depth and comprehensive explanations allow candidates fully understand the reason for why they are wrong and best books must provide fully explained tips and techniques to improve. There are practice books that offer better explanations for a particular subtest than others. Have a look at reviews from previous customers to get an idea of how well the book explains problems, check out customer reviews on sites like Amazon.

#4. Preparation Strategies & Tips

There is a popular saying that goes 'work smart not hard', practising questions only familiarises you with the exam and won't significantly improve your score. The right preparation involves identifying your weakness, continually assessing your improvement and working on your reasoning skills regularly. Unfortunately, not many practice books cover preparation strategies in depth but do offer loads of valuable tips sprinkled throughout to assist with tackling each subtest.

Every year I review the most popular UKCAT practice books, for my latest picks check out the blog:

WWW.THEUKCATBLOG.COM/RECOMMENDED-UKCAT-BOOKS/

Online UKCAT Courses

Online courses are a great investment, they replicate the testing environment and provide a bank of UKCAT questions. The best courses include learning materials to further aid with preparing for the test. I strongly recommend investing in one and using it throughout the duration of your preparation.

Though it is not mandatory, it can give you an edge in the exam. Practising questions in an online course factors into account the testing environment as well as pressure, both of which can influence your score significantly.

When using this type of resource be sure time yourself throughout the entire process, get familiar with the time limitations and pressures in the exam.

Pay attention to same KPIs as the UKCAT book stage, as well as your Speed. The time limitations in the exam are very challenging, so online courses are a great way to get used to the timing and honing your exam techniques accordingly.

Monitor your speed during practice, aim to complete each subtest within the set time. If you can't, figure out why - There is usually a pattern, identify this and learn techniques to improve.

When monitoring your speed, pay attention to the type of questions that take you longer to answer, and the mental processes that take you time. For example, it could be your slow at converting units in the quantitative reasoning section, to improve this you could learn shortcuts to go from, say Km/hr to m/s; and include it in your game plan for the exam. When I took the UKCAT, I discovered this was an issue when dealing with speed-distance-time questions so learned a few shortcuts to save time.

BONUS TIPS

Advice on Picking an Online UKCAT Course

The UKCAT is a computer-based exam so online courses that provide UKCAT practice questions are a must-have in preparing for the exam. There are a growing number of companies providing online courses so how do you pick the best one? The following are KEY factors to take into consideration when picking an online UKCAT course:

#1. Number of Practice Questions & Mocks

The more questions an online course offers the better, but make sure the quality of questions is great.

You want to pick an online course that covers the same breadth and depth of questions you can expect in the exam. A great way to find this out is buy looking on forums such as The Student Room or speaking with past applicants that have used the course you are enquiring about.

#2. Learning Feature

The most popular online UKCAT courses are including online tutorials and additional preparation material to help with preparing for the UKCAT. These resources usually include examples, explanations, and techniques for answering the various kinds of questions you can expect in the UKCAT in the form of video tutorials. The idea is that you learn exam techniques to later put into practice when you attempt their question bank.

#3. Simulation Feature

The UKCAT is a 2-hour test so it is natural anxiety, stress and fatigue could influence your score. However, the more you practice under real life conditions the less likely these factors will affect you on the live test. Online courses provide full-length mock exams to simulate the testing environment. The mocks should feel like the actual UKCAT, helping you experience the real test before your big day.

#4. Third Party Customer Feedback & Reviews

There are some bad online courses out there, so be sure to check customer reviews before making your final pick. If you can get a recommendation from a past applicant that would be ideal. If not, check on forums and third-party review sites.

#5. Pricing Flexibility

The flexibility of the pricing package is also an important factor, some companies offer flexibility in the pricing, where you can pay for a 2-week package or 1-month package etc, whilst some offer only one fixed package.

Depending on your plans and how soon you want to take the UKCAT it is a factor to take into consideration.

#7. UKCATSEN Supported

If you intend on taking the UKCATSEN then you want to ensure the course you pick is UKCATSEN supported. Not every online course offer this.

Every year I review and shortlist the best online UKCAT courses, for my latest picks check out the blog:

WWW.THEUKCATBLOG.COM/RECOMMENDED-ONLINE-UKCAT-COURSE/

UKCAT Crash Courses

UKCAT Crash courses can give you the edge because you are learning directly from experienced professionals. They provide real-time advice and strategies to improve your reasoning skill. Usually 1 to 2 days long where you are put through a series of exercises to help identify and improve skills.

Crash courses are great when you are consistently targeting weakest areas.

However, it is important that these courses are used smartly. I recommended before attending a course take the time to identify your weakest subtest beforehand (Step 3), once you've identified this, make it a priority on the day of your course and learn as many tips and techniques as possible from the UKCAT tutors. You want to squeeze out as much advice as possible. I wouldn't recommend focusing on all sections equally, make your two weakest sections the priority. I remember when I attempted the UKCAT the second time, I paid for a 2-day UKCAT crash course, overall it was good as it focused on all the sections of the exam, but in hindsight, I would've preferred to have spent those two days working on my two weakest subtests, verbal reasoning and quantitative reasoning.

Unfortunately, I didn't take full advantage of the course, I did no prior preparation so had no clue what I needed to improve, so it is no surprise my UKCAT score didn't improve much.

BONUS TIP

Advice on Picking a UKCAT Crash Course

The following are KEY factors to consider when picking a crash course to prepare for the UKCAT:

#1. Course Structure

The structure of the course is important, understand the areas being covered and how much time is being spent on each section. Wil there be a live mock? Or series of practice tests sprinkled throughout the day? Is the course interactive or not? You want to get a good grasp of the course structure and decide which is best for you.

#2. Additional Resources

There is a growing number of courses offering ongoing support after the course. These resources include access to thousands of practice questions, online lectures, email support and UKCAT books. Stay on the lookout for these additional resources.

#3. Third Party Reviews & Testimonials

UKCAT crash courses are not cheap, so you want to make sure you are getting your money's worth, a good way to do this is by checking past reviews and testimonials from past students. Have post on forums like The Student Room and Reddit to get recommendations and reviews.

Every year I review the most popular UKCAT crash courses, for my latest picks check out the blog:

UKCAT Tuition

Individual tuition provides one-on-one teaching tailored to you to give maximum improvement. In addition to the complete flexibility, another significant advantage is amount of time you spend practising – because there are no other students, you get much more opportunity to target your weak areas, building your skill and fluency in responding to the UKCAT questions. I recommend consistently targeting your weak areas throughout the duration of your tuition. Depending on your tutors teaching method aim to have a main subtest focus each week starting with your weakest subtest until you are comfortable with it.

BONUS TIP

Advice on Picking A UKCAT Tutor

I recommend taking the following into consideration when hiring a tutor:

#1. Teaching Method

The principles and methods used by tutors to enable learning is important. These strategies should be determined partly by you. Which teaching method works best for you? For example, some might offer weekly exercises to challenge you or others might kick off with a mock then break it down over a month to teach you core techniques for the exam. So, make to fully understand the method of teaching.

#2. Preparation Guidance

How closely will the tutor guide your preparation? The structure of each session plays an influence on this, most tutors encourage independent work acting to consolidate and enhance your skills. By suggesting reading materials, setting exercises and key areas to improve on, thus ensure you get the most return out of your independent time as well as sessions.

#3. Additional Support

There are companies that offer UKCAT Tuition, in additional to selecting one of their tutors you get access to additional resources such as online lectures, books and practice questions to consolidate your skills.

#4. Third Party Reviews & Testimonials

UKCAT tuition is expensive, so be sure to check past reviews and testimonials from past students. Get recommendations or see feedback on third party sites.

#5. Flexibility

You might have other commitments that may restrict your availability, so create a schedule beforehand and make sure it is fine with your potential tutor.

Every year I review the best UKCAT tutors, for my latest picks check out the blog:

WWW.THEUKCATBLOG.COM/RESOURCES/UKCAT-TUTORS/

Sub-Strategy for Each Subtest

The following are a breakdown of the practice sub-strategy for each subtest. **Do not read it in the order I have laid out**, start with your weakest section then move onto the next weakest one and so on.

Practice Sub-Strategy for Verbal Reasoning

Stage 1: Official Practice Test & Questions

Use free resources such as the official UKCAT practice questions and tests to identify the following:

- The verbal skill you struggle with the most e.g. comprehension or critical thinking
- Question types you find difficult
- Error Rate (un-timed conditions)
- Evaluate the verbal strategies and techniques

Stage 2: UKCAT Practice Books

Attempt more verbal questions and the verbal subtest in mock tests in practice books untimed. Spend more time practising and evaluating the question types you struggle with the most. Do not time yourself when attempting questions in these books, just focus on improving your error rate (aim to keep it below 20%). Feel free to explore other resources to improve weak areas.

Stage 3: Online UKCAT Course

Put strategies and tactics to practice by attempting questions under timed conditions with an online course. The UKCAT is a computer-based test so the most effective way to hone these skills is with an online course. Pay attention to your error rate, speed, question-type analysis and game plan. It is expected your error rate will get worse as you move from book to online, so do not worry, focus on improving it and keeping it below 30%.

Stage 4: Mock Subtest or Exam (Attempt Mock Exam After practising at least 2 subtests)

Once you have enough practice adopting your strategies. It's time to see how well you have improved. Attempt a mock subtest or exam with an online course and record your UKCAT score.

Use conversion table in the blog to calculate subtest score out of 900 or exam score out of 3600. Compare results to target score, last year's UKCAT averages and your scores from identifying your weakness. Is there an improvement? If not, figure out why. Reflect and suggest ways to improve.

Stage 5: Reflect & Repeat

Repeat the sub-strategy again but be more specific with what you work on. For example, you might realise that you struggled on a specific question type in the verbal section when you took the mock. Instead of going through general verbal practice questions, re-evaluate that specific question-type and go through each practice stage again working on that specific question-type.

Please note that you can attend a crash course or use tutoring service at any stage just make sure to identify your weak areas beforehand.

Practice Sub-Strategy for Quantitative Reasoning

Stage 1: Official Practice Test & Questions

Use free resources such as the official UKCAT practice questions and tests to identify the following:

- Numerical skill you struggle with e.g. basic arithmetic, problem solving or speed.
- Numerical concepts you might need to brush up on e.g. graphs, probability etc.
- Error rate (under timed and untimed conditions).

Pay attention to your error rate, question-type analysis and game plan.

Stage 2: Practice Books & GCSE Resources

Attempt quantitative questions and mock subtests in practice books untimed to practice learned techniques and strategies.

If necessary, also spend time getting up to speed with popular numerical concepts using GCSE maths resources. Keep an eye on your error rate, question types analysis and game plan. Do not time yourself when attempting questions in these books, focus mostly on improving error rate. Feel free to use other resources to improve weak areas.

Stage 3: Online UKCAT Course

Once you've got more comfortable with quantitative questions, you can now work on speed and honing your exam techniques. Focus on mastering time-saving strategies (e.g. mental maths tricks, estimation and elimination) by attempting questions under timed conditions.

Step 4: Mock Subtest or Exam

Once you have enough practice adopting your strategies under timed conditions. It's time to see how well you have improved. Attempt a mock subtest or exam with an online course and record your UKCAT score. Use conversion table in the blog to calculate subtest score out of 900 or exam score out of 3600. Compare results to target score, last year's averages and official practice test scores. Is there an improvement? If not, figure out why. Reflect and suggest ways to improve

Stage 5: Repeat

Repeat the whole strategy again but be more specific with what you work on. For example, you might realise that you struggled on a key GCSE concept when you took the mock. Instead of going through the entire practice questions again, only go through those concepts you found difficult and try to go through each step again. If speed is a main problem I suggest learning numerical shortcuts or mental maths tricks to save time.

Practice Sub-Strategy for Abstract Reasoning Subtest

Stage 1: Official UKCAT Practice Test & Questions

Use the official UKCAT questions and tests to identify the following:

- Difficult question-types
- Techniques and strategies that work well
- Error rate (under timed and untimed conditions)

Stage 2: UKCAT Practice Book

Review performance in the official test and practice questions and learn from answer rationales. Spend time practising questions untimed. I recommend making your game plan the main focus when using practice books, figure out the best technique and strategies that work for you in finding patterns.

Stage 3: Online UKCAT Courses

Once you've got more comfortable with the abstract questions, you can now work on speed and practice time saving strategies. I recommend some helpful techniques in Step 4 of my preparation strategy.

Stage 4: Mock Subtest or Exam

Once you have enough practice adopting your strategies under timed conditions. It's time to see how well you have improved. Attempt a mock subtest or exam with an online course and record your UKCAT score. Use conversion table in the blog to calculate subtest score out of 900 or exam score out of 3600. Compare results to target score, last year's averages and your scores from identifying your weakness. Is there an improvement? If not, figure out why. Reflect and suggest ways to improve.

Step 5: Repeat

Repeat the whole sub-strategy again but be more specific with what you work on. Look for room for improvement and work on it in the next round.

Practice Sub-Strategy for Decision Making Subtest

Stage 1: Official Practice Test & Questions

Use free resources such as the official UKCAT practice questions and tests to identify the following:

- Strength of deductive reasoning skills
- Ability to evaluate argument
- Strength of statistical reasoning
- Testing speed under timed conditions

Monitor error rate, question-types and your game plan.

Stage 2: Practice Books

Attempt decision making questions and mock subtests in practice books untimed to practice learned techniques and strategies. If necessary, spend time improving your puzzle and deductive techniques. Keep an eye on your error rate, question types and game plan. Do not time yourself when attempting questions in these books, focus mostly on improving error rate. Feel free to use other resources to improve weak areas.

Stage 3: Online UKCAT Course

Once you've got more comfortable with decision questions, work on speed and honing your exam techniques. Focus on master time-saving strategies by attempting questions under timed conditions.

Step 4: Mock Subtest or Exam

Once you have enough practice adopting your strategies under timed conditions. Attempt a mock subtest or exam with an online course and record your UKCAT score. Use conversion table in the blog to calculate subtest score out of 900 or exam score out of 3600.

Stage 5: Repeat

Repeat the whole strategy again but be more specific with what you work on. For example, you might realise that you struggled on logical puzzles. Instead of going through the entire decision subtest again, only go through the concept you found most difficult.

Practice Sub-Strategy for Situational Judgement

Stage 1: Official Practice Test & Questions

Use free resources such as the official UKCAT practice questions and tests to identify the following:

- Difficult question types

- Medical concepts and principles that may need revising

  Monitor error rate, question-types and game plan.

Stage 2: Practice Books & GMC documents

Attempt situational judgement questions in practice books untimed to practice learned techniques and strategies. I recommend reading the GMC *duties of a doctor's* guide and *tomorrows doctors* as well. Keep an eye on your error rate, question types and game plan. Do not time yourself when attempting questions in practice books, focus mostly on improving error rate. Feel free to use other resources to improve weak areas.

Stage 3: Online UKCAT Course

Once you've got more comfortable, you can now work on speed and honing your exam techniques. Focus on master time-saving strategies by attempting questions under timed conditions.

Step 4: Mock Subtest or Exam

Once you have enough practice adopting your strategies under timed conditions. Attempt a mock test.

Stage 5: Repeat

Repeat the whole strategy again, making your new weakest area the main focus.

The UKCAT 30 Day Study Plan

Included in the companion course is a 30-day study plan that incorporates both the preparation strategy and practice sub-strategy. It is designed to structure your preparation whilst using the core principles in this guide. The plan assumes you are working 3 hours per day.

Day 1 to Day 3 – *Identify weak areas (Step II)*

Attempt the official practice test. Do one practice test per day and review answer straight afterwards. Compile brief notes from your post-test analysis. Record the question-types you struggled with in each section, also pay attention to your processing speed and included suggestions to improve.

Day 4 - *Prioritize (Step III)*

Identify your true weakness in the UKCAT and prioritise the subtests accordingly. Review post-test notes and design game plan for each section. Pick at least three techniques and strategies you wish to adopt for each section to improve.

Day 5 to Day 9 – *Improve, Practice and Re-assess*

Day 5 to Day 9 should focus on improving your two weakest sections. Practice questions using books and online course. Practice using strategies and exam techniques to improve score then re-assess progress by Day 7 by attempting a mock subtest or set of questions under timed conditions and review performance. Suggest improvements and work on it Day 8 -9.

Day 10 – *Mock Exam 1*

Attempt a fully timed mock with no distractions. I recommend using an online UKCAT course to mimic the testing environment. Record results and compare to target score and UKCAT averages.

Day 11 to Day 14 – *Prioritise and Improve*

Using results from Mock test 1, identify areas for improvement (e.g.

question-types, skill and concepts) and learn techniques to improve them. Make your two weakest subtests priority. Remember your lowest subtest isn't necessarily your weakest.

Day 15 – *Mock test 2*

Attempt second mock fully timed and review answers. Record results and compare to Mock test 1 and UKCAT averages.

Day 16 to Day 19 – *Prioritise and Improve*

Using results from Mock test 2, identify question-types and elements you struggled on and work on improving them.

Day 20 – *Mock Test 3*

Attempt third mock fully timed and review answers.

Day 21 to Day 25 – *Prioritise and Improve*

Using results from Mock test 3, identify question-types and elements you struggled on and work on improving them.

Day 26 – Day 30 – *Review study notes & tie up loose ends*

Go through study notes and run through entire exam. I recommend having another look at the official practice questions and tests. Take the time to go through Mock exams again and probably do one final Mock if time permits.

Studying Hacks to Boost Productivity & Focus During Practice

1. Hacking Akrasia

Akrasia is a term that goes back centuries, it is essentially a lack of command over oneself, acting against your better judgment. An example of this may be spending hours watching YouTube videos when you are behind on your UKCAT preparation. Akrasia encompasses procrastination, lack of self-control, lack of follow-through, and any kind of addictive behaviour. You know what needs to be done but instead you do something else that adds no value to short term goals. The way you can hack Akrasia or avoid falling victim to it is two-fold:

- **Use a commitment Device:** A commitment device is essentially something you put in place to 'lock you in' to a certain course of action in the future, in this case preparing for the UKCAT. Bind yourself in getting a task done on time by using applications that limit distractions and/or force you to commit to your preparation.

There are plenty of great apps you can use to reduce Akasia from your digital environment and help you commit to more productive studying:

- Freedom is an app for Mac that allows you to lock yourself away from the Internet, so you can become more productive.
- StayFocusd is a Chrome extension that allows you to restrict the amount of time you can spend on time-wasting websites.
- Forest is a clever way to stay off your phone when you should be working. The app lets you plant a digital tree whenever you want to focus. The tree will then grow during the next 30 minutes, but if you leave the app, the tree will die. Stay committed and you'll plant a forest.
- News Feed Eradicator for Facebook is a Chrome extension that replaces your Facebook news feed with an inspiring quote.
- SelfControl is an app for Mac that lets you block your access to sites and mail servers for a set amount of time.
- Pact App — Allows you to create weekly pacts to study more and decide what you'll pay other Pact members if you fail. If you stay on track, you'll earn cash from other who didn't.

- **Short term Reward:** Give yourself short term rewards every time you hit a milestone in your preparation, it could be a snack or an episode of your favourite TV show, for example. Make sure that the reward isn't too far to attain that it causes Akrasia.

2. Pomodoro Technique

Research shows that studying is more effective in small short chunks rather than long sessions. For example, rather than doing 5 hours straight do 25 minutes chunks with five-minute rest in between. It is much more effective to break it down this way because your brain is better at encoding information into the synapses in short repeated sessions as opposed to one large one. Furthermore, studies show that after prolonged study sessions, reasoning and memory may be negatively affected for up to **FOUR WHOLE DAYS**!

The Pomodoro studying technique is a great way to get over this problem and improve productivity. It also great for beating procrastination and maintaining focus while preparing for the UKCAT.

The technique involves uses a timer to break down work into intervals, traditionally 25 minutes in length, separated by short 5 minutes breaks.

Step 1: Choose your task(s)

Step 2: Set timer for 25 minutes

Step 3: Work - Limit distractions for the entire 25 minutes. Do not be checking Facebook or your phone. Avoid all distractions at all cost!
Step 4: When timer goes off take 5 minutes break away from study area

Step 5: After 4 cycles take a longer break of 20 minutes.

You can modify the technique according to what works for you. I personally use 50/10 cycle where I work for 50 minutes straight and then rest for 10 minutes and repeat three to four times.

3. Simulate Testing Conditions

Simulate the testing environment as much as you can when you're studying. This means practising questions on a computer and simulating the time constraints as well. This will prime your brain beforehand and help reduce test anxiety.

4. Study Sessions While on A Walk

Try doing at least one study session while outside on a walk. Numerous studies show that when doing physical activity while your outside, the brain makes better connections, but you're getting an additional benefit as well. While you're outside you can see problems from a different perspective. Try practising questions on the official UKCAT app when walking to school for instance. The app is available on both IOS and Android devices.

Step 6: Assess

Assessing Your Performance

Three years ago, I was recommended a book by an old friend from sixth form, who had quit his job at the time to start a photography business. James was very passionate about capturing moments, his attention to detail when describing cameras and lens would have a regular person like myself muddled. His obsession with cameras matched his love of *anime* (Japanese animation). Don't get him started on 'Attack on Titans', a popular Japanese manga series he relentlessly recommended I watch for years before I eventually gave in, and now I'm a huge fan myself. Nonetheless, despite how well-versed he was in photography, he admitted that he had been struggling to manage his time running his business until reading a book titled the ***4-hour work week*** by Tim Ferriss.

I was struggling with balancing my time with managing the blog and he recommended this book. He was able to convince me to watch a Japanese animation I never thought in a million years I would watch four times over again, so thought I'd give his book recommendation a chance and I must admit it changed my life forever as well. The book covers a wide range of principles around building wealth whilst freeing up time. There is a particular principle that can be applied to preparing for the UKCAT, and it is called the 'Pareto Law' or the 'Pareto Distribution', popularly called the '80/20 Principle'.

Pareto Law can be summarized as follows: 80% of an output results from 20% of the input. The principle is named after Vilfredo Pareto, an economist, who in 1906 noticed that 80% of the land in Italy was owned by 20% of the population. The mathematical formula he used to demonstrate this distribution also applied to almost everything. Eighty percent of Pareto's garden peas were produced by 20% of the peapods he had planted, for example. This distribution became popular because it occurred over and over again in numerous scenarios, and it is still widely applied worldwide by companies, economists and governments, for example:

- About 20% of the world's population controls about 80% of the world's income.
- You would wear about 20% of the clothes in your wardrobe about 80% of the time.
- About 20% of a business's customers account for 80% of complaints.
- About 20% of your studying will lead to 80% of the outcome of your result.

The list is infinitely long and diverse. After learning about this principle, I began applying it to my own life and the blog, I even went as far as dissecting my UKCAT preparation strategy, through the lens of one single question:

What 20% of my preparation strategy caused 80% of my desired UKCAT score?

For an entire weekend, I put everything aside and did the most truth-baring analysis possible. I even spoke with successful candidates who had bought the first edition of the study guide in order to validate my claims and find inefficiencies in the strategy. Even though I'm aware that the 80/20 principle isn't a universal law that occurs in all situations, it is an effective rule of thumb to analyse your preparation and be more productive.

- Which 20% of exam strategies improved my accuracy or error rate by 80%

- Which 20% of techniques improved my speed in each subtest by 80%

- Which 20% combination of tips, techniques and strategies improved my mock results by 80%

In other words, seek and focus on the 20% of work that will result to 80% of your desired UKCAT outcome. This will vary with every candidate, but to help ensure you are on the right track I have introduced key performance indicators (KPI) to help monitor performance to make it easier to apply the 80/20 principle.

The UKCAT Preparation KPIs

A key performance indicator (KPI) is a type of measurement that evaluates progression over time. It is widely used by businesses to monitor and analyse factors deemed crucial to the success of an organization.

We will adopt this concept to assess our performance against a set of targets. By setting KPIs it enables you make smarter decisions about the direction of your revision and apply the Pareto law effectively. Often success in an exam like the UKCAT is simply the repeated, periodic achievement of micro study goals.

Accordingly, choosing the right KPIs relies upon a good understanding of what is important to smash the exam.

> Success in an exam like the UKCAT is simply the repeated, periodic achievement of micro study goals.

Measuring and monitoring your performance is critical but focusing on the wrong performance indicators can be detrimental. So can poorly structured KPIs, or KPIs that are too difficult to monitor on a regular basis. To be useful, KPIs must be monitored and be actioned on immediately, in this chapter we will discuss the five KPIs to monitor during preparation and how to assess them using Pareto law:

1. Error Rate

Error rate refers to the frequency at which you answer questions incorrectly within a specific subtest. It is measured as a percentage and can be calculated using the formula below:

$$\text{E. R} = \frac{Total\ number\ of\ incorrect\ responses}{Total\ questons\ attempted} \times 100$$

This metric is a good way to monitor your accuracy over time as you practice exam questions. I recommend calculating your error rate for each subtest after every mock exam as seen below.

Calculating error rate is also useful when attempting questions in practice books untimed. Track your error rate when you do mini-tests or exercises within these resources. Focus on improving your accuracy. I recommend aiming to keep you error rate below 20% when attempting questions.

Subtests	Error Rate (%)		
	Mock 1	**Mock 2**	**Mock 3**
Verbal Reasoning			
Quantitative Reasoning			
Abstract Reasoning			
Decision Making			
Situational Judgement			

2. Speed

Speed is a measure of how quickly you complete a subtest within its time limitations. This is an important KPI that must be monitored during every timed exercise. I strongly recommend reflecting on your use of time in each section after attempting mini-tests and mocks.

UKCAT Subtests			
Subtest	**Time Allowed**	**Number of Questions**	**Time Per Question**
Verbal Reasoning	21 minutes	44	30 seconds
Quantitative Reasoning	24 minutes	36	38 seconds
Abstract Reasoning	13 minutes	55	15 seconds
Decision Making	31 minutes	29	64 seconds

Situational Judgement	26 minutes	69	22 seconds

The table above is the timing for each section. I also included a breakdown of the *time per question* for those who may decide to time themselves during practice with a resource that doesn't include a timing component. For instance, you may want to work on your speed by timing yourself when practising abstract questions in a book. If you set a mini-test of 20 questions then you would aim to complete it in 5 minutes.

$$\text{Time } (mins) = \frac{No \ of \ Questions \times Time \ per \ Question}{60}$$

i.e.

$$\text{Time (mins)} = \frac{20 \times 15}{60} = 5 \ mins$$

Therefore, the total time to complete a 20-question abstract reasoning mini-test is 5 minutes.

3. Mock Test Analysis

Mock tests are a vital component of my preparation strategy. I recommend doing at least three mock exams before your big day under timed conditions and analysing the results. The analysis should include the following:

- Comparison between mock test score and UKCAT average score for previous year.
- Comparison between mock test score and minimum target score
- Comparison between mock test score and previous mock test
- Identification of your weakest subtest (remember it is not necessarily your lowest score)

Once you have assessed each component develop an action plan to improve. This analysis will help you see how close you are to achieving your target score with every mock completed.

	vs Average	vs Target	vs Previous Mock	Weakest Subtest
Mock Test 1			N/A	
Mock Test 2				
Mock Test 3				

Each component (except for the weakest subtest) is expressed as a percentage. For example, let's say you scored 2650 in Mock Test 1 and 2840 in mock test 2, in the Mock test 2 *'vs previous mock'* box you would put **+ 5.2%,** explaining that your overall score has increased by 5.2%.

4. Question Type Analysis

This is an additional layer of analysis when exploring exercises. It is an evaluation of the type of questions you find difficult in each section of the UKCAT. The aim is to find your weak areas within a subtest. For example, when I prepared for the UKCAT I realised the verbal reasoning section was my weakest, see below my question-type analysis report.

Subtest	Question-Type	Analysis
Verbal Reasoning	True/False or Can't Tell	Strongest (best error rate)
	Incomplete Statements	2nd Weakest
	According To The Passage	3rd weakest

	Except Question	Weakest (worst error rate)
	Most Likely	2nd strongest

I broke down the subtest into its question-types and worked out my error rate for each one. The question type I answered most correctly was my strongest and the question-type I answered the most incorrectly was my weakest. Using the results from my analysis I spent more time practising **except questions** and **incomplete statement** questions during verbal practice and learned strategies to improve my accuracy for each one.

5. Game Plan Evaluation

An evaluation of how well the tips, techniques and strategies you've adopted improved your results. The game plan should be split into two categories - accuracy and speed.

Accuracy: These are the tips, techniques and strategies that improve accuracy and error rate.

Speed: These are the tips, techniques and strategies that improve your speed.

It is important to note that each subtest will have its own game plan. For instance, the techniques you adopt to save time in the verbal reasoning section will be different from the strategies used to save time in the quantitative reasoning subtest. I strongly recommend during practice to try as many strategies as possible until you've found a set of techniques that significantly improve your accuracy and speed. It could be a combination of techniques; the idea is that you have this planned out beforehand. During the live test, remind yourself these strategies during the 1-minute instruction section before each subtest. Find below my game plan evaluation for the verbal reasoning section:

Subtest	Question-Type	Game Plan
Verbal Reasoning	True/False or Can't Tell	*Keyword Strategy*
	Incomplete Statements	*Keyword Diary & Mapping*
	According to The Passage	*Keyword Diary & Mapping*
	Except Question	*Elimination & Keyword Strategy*
	Most Likely	*Elimination Technique*

Without a proven game plan my chances of smashing the exam would have been slim. I identified what worked for me and improved the speed at which I implemented them. Also pay attention to your **mental processing speed**, there might be concepts that take you a while to calculate, for example - basic arithmetic or calculating percentages in the quantitative section, try to learn shortcuts or mental techniques to help with solving them quicker. I remember I learned very helpful shortcuts for converting km/hr to m/s for speed distance and time problems that proved very valuable on test day.

"What gets measured gets managed"

- Peter Drucker

The key to successfully applying the Pareto law is by making the most of the 20% of your time that will produce 80% of your results. The entire preparation strategy is designed with this in mind and makes sure you are working efficiently and effectively by:

- Narrowing down the strategies and techniques that work for you

- Making your revision more specific as you prepare for the exam

Using KPIs ensures you spend a majority of your preparation time working on your weakest areas, then moving on to the next weakest subtest (or question type) once you have improved or become more comfortable with it.

To improve, every aspect of preparation must have a **feedback loop**. During assessment, KPIs reveal essential data to help develop feedback and create an effective action plan for attacking weak areas. However, this is only effective if the above KPIs are monitored on a regular basis.

The 'Improve – Assess' Loop

When working on a specific concept (e.g. Venn diagram questions) it may be better to shorten the strategy into an *'improve-assess'* cycle as seen below. Read resources and take mini-tests to improve knowledge and assess skill. Once you feel comfortable with the concept, take a mock or mini-test and re-assess progress. If you are happy with the results, move onto the next concept and start preparation cycle from the beginning (i.e. Identify).

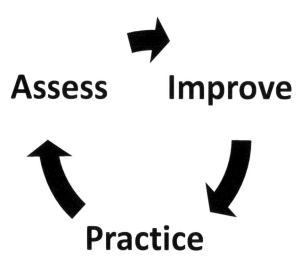

I want to reiterate that the 80/20 principle should be used as a rule of thumb when picking strategies and figuring out what component of each subtest should be priority.

For perfectionists out there reading this, I want to make it clear that obsessing over achieving a perfect score or an error rate below 20% before moving to the next question-type or subtest will not only waste time but hinder your improvement. Do not waste time obsessing over not hitting your target. They've been hundreds of success stories of candidates who never hit their target score during preparation and went on to surpass it by up to 40%.

Perceived Comfort vs KPI Results

Rather than working on one specific question type until you've hit your goal (say an error rate of 15%), move on to the next weakest area once you feel more comfortable. There are instances where you may feel comfortable with a concept but still achieve below target or perform worse than previously. This inconsistency is expected and, in such instances, do not panic, try to figure out what element(s) needs improvement, give yourself a break and return back to that it.

Instead of feeling anxious or uncertain about "where you stand," look for ways to turn score inconsistencies into valuable learning:

Look for what was significant about low vs high scoring days

Was there a particular issue on a day of a low score such as fatigue or ability to focus? Did you feel particularly good on days when you got higher scores? Look for clues as to what daily habits (sleep, stress, caffeine intake) affect your performance. You'll want to optimize these for test day.

Address low vs high scoring content

Was there a substantial difference in what was tested from one test to another? Perhaps you were more/less familiar with the topics covered in a couple passages on a single test in a way that impacted the outcome. Variation in test content can happen, so take notes of what concept you should be focusing more on.

You can immediately and significantly improve the potency of your practice taking by simply doubling back and reviewing each practice test as you take it. By being attentive to why you chose both correct and incorrect answers, you can catch problematic approaches to passages and questions that may be leading you to miss questions on material you know or only luckily mark a correct answer choice when you do not truly understand. In addition, you are solidifying that knowledge in the context of how it may be applied.

Keep track of your perceived and performed strengths and weaknesses. Do you see improvement on a topical level over time and across practices tests?

Practice test scores can go up and down. What matters is how you perform on test day. Use your practice tests to your advantage by taking lessons from each experience — be it test-taking skills or identifying strengths and weakness — and use what you learn to adjust your prep both in terms of content review and daily habits. Look to each practice test, regardless of its score, as an opportunity to reflect on your progress and make adjustments. Understanding how you got to a low (or high!) practice test score may help ease the uncertainty of inconsistent performance. Then you can apply that understanding and get back to work!

Best from the Blog

1.

Best time to take the UKCAT

As a former UKCAT candidate that took the exam three times, I know a thing or two about booking the UKCAT exam. Registration and booking for the UKCAT opens in May. In this article I'll be offering advice on the best time to book your test. If you plan on taking the UKCAT, you should already be aware that you are free to take the test anytime between July to October, but when is the best time to take the test?

The Short answer: The Best Time to Take the UKCAT Is Subjective

Most students take the UKCAT at the end of the Summer, in either August or September. This is probably due to the fact that summer is a busy time. Many students will either be working or enjoying a break from their studies.

Some students might be travelling for part or all of the summer. Depending on your personal plans, there are any number of factors that could impact your decision on when to sit the UKCAT. You can select any date from July 1st to October 5th to take the test, depending on availability at your preferred test centre. Thus, the choice is really up to you. My advice is to consider factors that might affect your preparation or performance on the test day and schedule your test appointment appropriately. Since you can choose any available test appointment, there is no reason not to choose the appointment that will give you the greatest advantage.

Factors to Consider Before Booking Your Test

The following are factors to consider before booking your UKCAT test:

1. Will you be working in the summer?

If you are working or volunteering, then you might need longer time to prepare for the exam. I recommend setting up study schedule, to ensure that you will have sufficient time to revise and practise before your test. Depending on your working hours, you might want to schedule your test for later in the summer.

2. Will you be travelling, whether for a week or two or even longer?

If you have travelling plans, how realistic is it for you prepare for the UKCAT? You might find it challenging to get a bit of space and quiet to revise and practise for the UKCAT whilst on holiday. Taking a practice test in one sitting (and being able to concentrate, even for a bit of quick practice) could be very difficult indeed. If a vacation is on the cards, then you might want to consider delaying your UKCAT preparation until after the holiday.

Depending how long you are away for you could consider getting up to speed by attending a UKCAT seminar upon your return, with your test appointment to follow 2 to 4 weeks later.

3. Are You Taking the BMAT or GAMSAT?

If you are planning on taking the BMAT (in November) or GAMSAT (in September) then you might want to schedule your test early in the summer to give you time to prepare for the other exams.

4. How Prepared Are You?

I recommend booking your test depending on how easy you find the official UKCAT practice tests. If you score well and find it easy, I reckon 4 – 8 weeks is enough preparation. However, if you achieve a low score I recommend giving yourself longer.

5. How much time do you need To Prepare?

I personally do not think you need longer than 2 months to prepare for the exam. Typically, students take between 2 weeks to a month to prepare for the UKCAT. Attempt the official UKCAT practice tests first then set a date depending on how easy you find it. If you find it easy 2 - 4 weeks should be enough. However, if you find it difficult you may need longer.

6. What's the best time of day for your test appointment?

The options to take the UKCAT range from early morning – as early as 8am — to late in the afternoon — as late as 3 or 4pm, depending on the test centre. I strongly advise you consider past experiences taking tests; when are you the sharpest? A study recently published concluded that students are at the height of their cognitive abilities in the morning and perform better at exams. Remember, the UKCAT will be a very intense 2 hours of staring at a monitor, while working incredibly quickly through a wide range of question types and completing over 200 questions without a break, so you want to be at your best.

2.

What to do if you achieve a low UKCAT score?

et me start by saying that achieving a low UKCAT score isn't the end of the world. It just means you might have fewer options available. Universities with a high cut-off mark are obviously not an option to apply. However, a UKCAT score below the cut-off of one medical or dental school may be good enough for admittance to another. The following six things I recommend you do if you achieve a low UKCAT score:

1. Find Out Your Decile Rank

The UKCAT exam board uses a statistical approach called deciles to report the overall performance of candidates each year. A decile is any of nine values that divide data into ten equal parts so that each part represents 10% of the sample population. This statistical approach is descriptive and gives the exam board a good overview of the overall test performance each year. I recommend finding out where your overall score ranks before applying. It could be that the year you take the UKCAT it is difficult and most students find it hard as well. This could potentially put you in a higher decile. You ideally want to be in the 6th decile and above. Applicants below the 4th decile are normally rejected before the interview stage.

2. Consider Universities that use a Point-based System

If you score a low UKCAT score I recommend you research all the universities and find out how they each assess the UKCAT, you want to shortlist universities that do not have a cut-off mark or have a cut off below your achieved score. Shortlist universities that also use a point-based system when picking applicants to interview and lay more emphasis on the entire application when shortlisting applicants i.e. predicted grades, work experience, reference, personal statement etc.

Once you have shortlisted the universities I recommend giving their admissions team a call, I cover this in detail in the next step.

3. Call Admission Tutors for More Information

Let's assume you've found seven universities that do not have a cut-off or use a point-based system. You want to get an idea on how heavily they rely on the UKCAT. The best way to find out is by calling their admissions team. Here are a few questions you could ask:

→ How heavily do you rely on the UKCAT?

→ How are applicants shortlisted for interview?

→ What was the average UKCAT score for applicants you interviewed last year?

→ What was the lowest UKCAT score from last year's interview pool?

→ What do you consider a good UKCAT score?

The admissions team's answer to these questions will give you a rough indication on how much they rely on the exam and the likelihood of you being invited for an interview. You want to shortlist four universities that will most likely invite you for an interview.

4. Strengthen Other Parts of Application

To give yourself the best possible chance of being invited for an interview you need to strengthen other parts of your application. There are a few things you could do to give you a bit of an edge:

→ Show individual marks to modules on your UCAS application, show the marks of your highest scoring modules, GSCE subjects, etc

→ Personal Statement – Highlight your commitment to a career in medicine and what you've learned from work experience. Try to stand out in whatever way you can.

→ Provide a reference from someone in a medical or dental profession.

→ Review your letter of recommendation – make sure all the attributes the university is looking for is highlighted by your referee. Ask your referee to also include an example of when you've demonstrated these skills in the letter.

5. Consider BMAT or GAMSAT Universities

There are many medical and dental programmes that do not require the UKCAT as part of their application process. I would recommend taking the time to also research these options, they might actually be a more suitable or an easier route for you to study medicine or dentistry.

6. Consider Alternative Routes

There is more than one route to medicine or dentistry, for instance – you could consider graduate medicine or dentistry with a foundation year. There are alternative routes to both courses. One of my friends actually studied nursing at university before getting into medicine and I have another mate that did Biomedical Sciences before getting a place on the dental programme at King's College. These routes might be longer but will strengthen your application if you've achieved a high grade or degree class.

3.

Is the UKCAT Hard?

L ast year I created a poll on the private Facebook UKCAT Study Guide and asked students How hard they found the UKCAT? Check out the results from the poll:

As you can see in the screenshot beloe, I gave students 6 options to pick from, they included:

- Very Easy

- Easy

- Easy - OK

- OK

- Hard

- Very Hard

From the students that responded to the poll. 41% of students thought the exam was OK, 35% thought it was HARD, about 12% thought it was EASY-OK. 6% thought it was VERY HARD and another 6% thought it was EASY.

I hope the results of the poll, does not put you off taking the test, because it shouldn't! with the right preparation you'll be fine.

4.

How to Pick Your Medical or Dental School

You probably have your ideal choices in mind but make sure to take the following factors into account before submitting your final application. When I first applied to medicine I only looked into entry requirements - I was predicted to achieve 3 A's. I was naive to think I would get at least an interview based on my predicted grades. I laugh at myself every time I look back because the year I applied there were 80,000 applicants for medicine, which meant that there were1-in-10 applicants per place. Medicine and Dentistry are so competitive, choosing a course largely based on thinking you will hit the entry requirements is not enough!

The following are some of the KEY factors I took into account when I began narrowing down my choices the third time I applied:

1. Course Structure & Teaching: This is the most important factor when picking your medical or dental school. I recommend you choose a university largely based on course structure and its teaching style.

2. UKCAT Assessment & Selection Process: Every university uses the UKCAT differently, some have cut-off makes whilst others use a scoring or point based system where they look at different components of one's application before deciding who to invite for interview. It is by understanding this process you can have a rough idea on how good your chances are of getting an interview. I actually cover this step-by-step in my UKCAT Study Guide, I explain how to use this understanding to set a target score during practice.

In fact, I would go as far as to say do not shortlist your choices until you have taken the UKCAT. I remember I shortlisted 12 universities when I applied, I had my 4 ideal choices if I did well in the test. Another 4 if I did OK and a final 4 if I didn't perform so well. In hindsight, it was a waste of time, I recommend narrowing down your final choices tactically after the UKCAT.

3. Application to Places Ratio: The third time I applied I went a little 'crazy'. I looked into how many places against the number of students that applied to get a rough idea of the competition. For example, let's say that 2000 students applied to Queen Mary, which has 250 places. Then the Application:Places ratio would be 8 i.e. 8 students were applying to every place. I don't recommend using this as the main criteria to shortlist but could be worth using if you have to decide between two universities that are equal in comparison.

I took all THREE factors into account when shortlisting my choices and ended up with 4 medical school interviews. It is worth taking the time to think tactically about where to apply don't just look at entry requirements.

5.

5 Biggest Mistakes I Made When I Applied

I want to share 5 Mistakes to avoid when picking your medical or dental school. These are some of the mistakes I initially made when I applied to Medicine the first time and was left with 4 rejections and no university place.

Here we go (be prepared to cringe) ...

1. Only Researching into Your Ideal 4 Choices

I appreciate you probably have 4 medical or dental schools picked out at this point. However, you need to keep an open mind when applying to these competitive courses. I remember when I first applied I only really looked into London medical schools because I wanted to live in London so badly, I didn't take the time to look into ALL the medical school programmes in the UK. I recommend researching into all the schools that offer your desired programme, find out their entry requirements, understand their selection process and how they assess the UKCAT. This will help you make a more informed decision when shortlisting your choices.

2. Not Fully Understanding Their Selection Process

It is not enough to just understand what the entry requirements are, look into the selection process of these course, i.e. take the time to find out how they shortlist applicants to invite for interview. Do they put more emphasis on academics or the UKCAT? Do they use a UKCAT cut-off? Finding this out helps you know how realistic your chances are of being invited for an interview. You can make smarter decisions with regards to the final 4 courses you decide to shortlist. Just a quick tip, do not settle for just the information provided on university website get more details by calling their admissions office and asking more direct questions like "what was the minimum UKCAT score for students you invited for interview last year" etc.

3. Only practising questions for the UKCAT

The UKCAT is a tough exam in my opinion, however, you can smash it if you prepare smartly. Just attempting questions with no real strategy isn't enough, you'll only end up familiarising yourself with the exam, not actually improving your reasoning skills. I recommend having a strategy for your preparation and developing an attack plan for each section of the exam.

4. Not focusing on "what I've learned" on my Personal Statement

I might as well just put it out there now, admission tutors care more about what you've learned from an experience. You can have 6 weeks placement at your local GP, if you do not mention what you've learned you are no different from the thousands of applicants that apply to their course. Be reflective on everything you mention on your personal statement. This makes a huge difference.

5. Not Keeping Your UCAS Referee up to date

This is overlooked by many students, keep your UCAS referee in the loop about everything you are doing to get into medicine or dentistry! Tell them about your volunteer experience, what you've learned, what you hate, etc! Basically, treat them like a HUMAN DIARY! meet with them regularly either biweekly or monthly.

I guarantee you they'll write a more compelling reference, backed up with examples of why they think you should be accepted into your desired course.

6.

10 Tips for Smashing the UKCAT

was able to achieve a UKCAT score in the 90th percentile! In this article I want to share with you how I did it. That's right! The following are my top 10 tips for smashing the UKCAT.

1. Set A Target Score During Preparation

Obviously you want to achieve the highest UKCAT score possible. However, you need to set a target practice score as this will act as a benchmark during preparation. Typically, this would be the minimum UKCAT score needed to be invited for an interview for your ideal choice. Universities assess the UKCAT differently, some have a total cut-off and whilst others do not have a cut-off at all. You need to find out how your choices assess the exam and set yourself an ideal and minimum target score based on your findings. After researching all my choices I decided to set a target score of 700 and a minimum of 650. This was the benchmark I set myself during my preparation. If I achieved below 650 average in a mock exam, I would consider it a fail. My entire preparation was based on beating that mark.

2. Identify Your Weakness first

Before buying any practice book or enlisting on any course, identify which sections of the UKCAT you find the most difficult. The UKCAT is made up of 5 subtests, they include Verbal reasoning, Abstract reasoning, Decision Making, Abstract Reasoning and Situational Judgement. The most reliable way to find out your weakness is by attempting the official practice tests on the UKCAT website, it is updated each year to reflect the same level of difficulty candidates can expect in the exam.

I recommend you attempt the tests before you start preparing for the exam, it'll help identify which areas you need to work on the most. I remember when I took the UKCAT I quickly discovered that the verbal reasoning subtest was my weakest section so I spent a majority of my preparation time learning and adopting new strategies to improve my verbal score.

3. Prioritise Smartly

A common mistake candidates make is that they can at times find themselves feeding their ego without even realising it, where they spend the majority of their time on sections of the exam they enjoy the most. This is a waste of time, think about it, if you find the Abstract reasoning section easier than verbal reasoning, it doesn't make sense to practice more abstract questions. Studies show that honing your strongest section only boosts your overall UKCAT score by 10-15% but focusing on your weakest section can boost your overall score by 20-30%. That is double the impact! Give priority to your weakest section and spend most of your preparation improving it. I spent 45% of my preparation time practising verbal questions (weakest section) and about 10% of my time practising my strongest section, which was the abstract section.

4. Practice 'Question-types' not just Sections

I took the UKCAT three times. I realised the second time I took the UKCAT my average score didn't improve by much despite practising thousands of questions. This is because practising questions only familiarises you with the exam, it doesn't significantly improve your reasoning skills. In order to really smash the UKCAT, you need to dig deeper! Try to understand which type of question in each subtest you struggle with. For instance, in the Abstract reasoning section there are four types of questions that examiners include, you might find one type of question difficult and another easy. It makes sense to focus your efforts on improving the one question-type you find most difficult instead of the entire abstract section.

5. Evaluate Your Progress

Another mistake to avoid is just practising questions after questions with no strategy, you must evaluate your progress throughout the duration of your preparation. A good way to evaluate your progress is by attempting a mock exam every week until your big day. After each mock exam compare your results with the previous one. This will help identify areas of improvement and ensure you are working effectively to boost your weakest skills. I remember when I took the exam I did a total of 5 mock exams before my big day. I noticed by the end of week 3 I had significantly improved my verbal reasoning score but my quantitative score hadn't improved much. So I spent a majority of the remaining weeks working on my quantitative skills.

6. Learn Exam Strategies to Compensate Weak Reasoning Skills

It is virtually impossible to significantly improve your cognitive skills in a short amount of time. For example, if you are a slow reader, you won't be able to significantly increase your reading speed in 2 weeks or a month. However, you can learn exam strategies and techniques to improve your ability to read and comprehend information quickly. I'm really slow at working out maths in my head, but I learned a few mental maths tricks to combat this problem so I can save time in the quantitative section.

7. Practice with an Online Course

The UKCAT is a computer-based test, you need to practice questions under the same exam conditions as the real test. Pick an online course that closely mimics the testing experience and allows you to familiarise yourself with the onscreen format of the exam. The best online courses contain answer items at the same equivalent standard as UKCAT and allow you review your responses against answer rationales. Online courses are also a great way to hone your exam strategies and techniques. There are loads of companies offering online courses so be sure to read reviews and customer feedback before choosing one.

8. Improve skill don't Just Practice

Practising questions only increase your familiarity with the exam. You need to also identify which elements or skills you struggle with and work on improving it. For instance, if you find the verbal section difficult this might be due to a number of things, you might have poor comprehension or critical thinking skills or possibly a slow reader. Try to identify what element you struggle with and try to improve it. I'm a naturally slow reader - in order to combat this, I spent a month before the test reading everything online and adopting strategies to comprehend information in the verbal section quicker.

9. Do A Mock Exam Every Week

There is no other better way to assess yourself than attempting mock exams. Treat them like the real test. Do an entire 2-hour test with no breaks and no distractions. I recommend attempting your mocks on an online course to mimic the testing environment.

10. Be Confident

My last tip, do not let your nerves get the better of you, with practice you'll become more confident. However, the combination of applying to university and sitting the UKCAT can be stressful but try to stay calm during your preparation – not only do you feel better, but also perform better.

7.

Got Rejected from Your Choices? Here Is What to Do

G etting rejected from all your choices is a horrible experience, I applied three times to medical school and got rejected by all my choices the first and second time. It had a serious knock on my confidence and I almost entirely gave up on pursuing a career in medicine. No one wants to have to apply a second time and definitely not a third time. After a second rejection, a lot of people recommended picking another field or even giving up altogether. For me, both of my rejections were hard and still to this day, I can recall the frustration and failure that I felt during those times. However, I believe getting rejected twice was one of the best things to happen to me. It was a true test of my passion for pursuing medicine. If you find yourself in a position where you've been rejected by all your choices these are five things I recommend you do to give yourself a better chance of getting in when you re-apply.

1. Focus on Achieving Your Predicted Grades

It is natural to feel disheartened or a bit depressed after you've received a rejection from your university choice. It can be hard to refocus your efforts on studying, most students get caught up in trying to get feedback on why they got rejected, this can at times distract them from their studies. Don't get caught up in the application process focus on achieving your predicted grades. This will give you a better chance when you re-apply. I remember constantly viewing my UCAS page for updates and proofreading my personal statement many times after I had applied. When you apply to medical school expect the worse possible outcome and focus on achieving your grades.

2. Do Not Waste Time Getting Feedback

I remember calling up my choices to find out why I got rejected. The representatives never gave specific advice. This is understandable when you consider the vast number of applicants that apply. Do not waste your time chasing feedback it is a lost cause.

Focus on achieving your predicted grades! I only recommend chasing for detailed feedback if you've had an interview, you are more likely to get specific feedback on your performance.

3. Speak to Your Academic Tutor (or Referee)

It is natural to feel embarrassed about the outcome, I didn't tell my friends or family till after a month. Instead of dealing with it alone speak with your tutor or teacher, they will be able to provide support and review your application on how to improve it. If you plan on reapplying let them know, they might be able to give you helpful advice.

4. Clearing

I'm personally not a big fan of clearing because in most cases students settle for any degree without really making an informed decision. However, St George's medical school announced it would open up places onto its medicine course through clearing for this first time ever in 2016. Around 40 places were on offer through the process, which was used by the university to fill up leftover places. It is highly competitive and be prepared for another interview round. This is a great option for those who have been rejected by their choices and didn't apply to St George's Medicine Programme but have achieved good grades (3A's and above). Clearing can also be used to get a place into health-related programmes such as biomedical science, paramedic science, Pharmacology or healthcare science, that provide a great platform for later getting into graduate Medicine or Dentistry.

5. Find Out Helpful Information from Admission Tutors

Instead of ringing up your choices to find out why you've been rejected, ask for more specific information. Find out the cut-off score for the UKCAT for the application cycle you applied, or how many students applied, what was the average UKCAT score of candidates who were accepted etc.

You can use the information to your advantage when you reapply. Knowing the cut-off mark for the UKCAT that year can help set a target score when you re-apply the following year.

6. Reflect Objectively

Once the dust has settled and you've finished your final exams reflect on your application. It is hard to reflect on your application immediately after you've been rejected. Try to think about how you can improve, really think about the shortfalls of your application and how you can improve it for next time if you decide to reapply. If you honestly think it's "perfect" show your application to a university advisor or academic tutor. They should be able to criticise your application to help you improve it.

8.

Developing a <u>SOLID</u> Back up Plan

I think it is important to develop a backup plan before applying to medical or dental school because they are highly competitive courses. UCAS requires all medical school applicants to pick a fifth choice that is an alternative degree. For some this might be alternative routes to medical school or dental school, for others it could be a completely different career path but I recommend considering the following to help develop your medical school backup plan.

1. What Am I Good At?

I know loads of students that went into Biomedical Sciences hoping they will get into graduate medicine later down the road. Make sure you are picking your fifth choice based on what you are good at, look into core modules, teaching styles and course structure. I remember when I was at the University of Manchester there were students that struggled with the chemistry modules of the course.

They just couldn't get their heads round the core chemistry principles they needed to apply to key Pharmaceutical concepts. I actually dated a girl on my course who hated chemistry and struggled with the chemistry concepts, but was very good with the physiology modules, she would have probably found it a lot easier if she stuck solely with her passion and studied Physiology instead. Take the time to really think about what you are good at, do not pick a fifth choice solely because it could potentially get you a place into graduate medicine or

dentistry later down the road.

2. What Do I enjoy?

In my opinion, this is the most important question you must ask yourself. Pick a fifth choice that you enjoy. You have to imagine that if a career in medicine or dentistry doesn't work out what would you rather do? What would you dedicate the next 4 years studying? Or maybe what other career would you consider? For some this might still be in the health sector for others it could be something completely different. I have a mate I studied with in Pharmacology that now runs a mobile app company that helps enhance cognitive function – combining both his passion in neuroscience and technology.

Remember that whatever you decide will take 3-4 years that's a really long time if you are not passionate.

3. What Are the Entry Requirements, Course Structure and Teaching Style?

Another consideration that makes a significant difference from one university to another is how you are taught and assessed. There are three main approaches: traditional, integrated and problem-based learning. Check out which approach your preferred choices use and consider if this suits the way you enjoy learning.

4. Should I take A Gap Year?

Taking a gap year can be tremendously beneficial to one's personal growth, whether one decides on enrolling in a structured gap year program, spend time volunteering abroad or simply traveling the world. Regardless, taking a gap year gives you the chance to think things through, do not rush into university if you aren't sure. I took a gap year and it was probably one of the smartest things I've ever done despite getting pressured from family to get into university. You can use the time to reflect on your achieved grades or get relevant work experience to enhance your application.

5. How Can I Make My Application Stronger?

This last point is really for those who are determined to get in medical or dental school if they do not make it the first time applying. I recommend you consider how you can make your application stronger the next time you reapply. For Instance, if you did not achieve the grades, you'll need to work hard enough to get a strong degree class in your backup choice.

BONUS EXERCISE!

#ASKMIKE

Well done on completing the UKCAT Study Guide!!

To show my appreciation you can win a FREE consultation call with me as part of the #ASKMIKE competition offered to 20 students every year, where I provide one-to-one consultation on preparing for the UKCAT, applying to medicine and improving your personal statement. Absolutely free!

Just visit the link below and fill in the form to enter!

I look forward to hearing from you! Best of Luck!

WWW.THEUKCATBLOG.COM/ASKMIKE

A Note from Mike

Thank you to all the fans of THEUKCATBLOG.COM - the readers that have motivated and supported me throughout the years.

I'm lucky to have an audience that aren't fazed by the uncertainty with our healthcare system and still want to dedicate the rest of their lives providing care to others, and for that I am truly hopeful. I will continue to serve you through the work that I do.

Thank you again for reading the UKCAT study guide. If you found it helpful please take a moment to leave a review at your favourite online retailer such as Amazon.

I welcome contact from readers as well, if you have any questions please do not hesitate to get in touch.

Best of luck in the exam!

Mike

Conversion Table

The conversion table will help identify your weakest subtest (Step 2). The scores are for approximation purposes only. Scores on the UKCAT are given in 10-point intervals, so actual scores will vary slightly. This table is designed to bark on the side of caution, so in most cases a similar performance on the UKCAT would result in a slightly higher score.

	Verbal Reasoning	Quantitative Reasoning	Abstract Reasoning	Decision Making
300	0 – 5	0 – 3	0 – 6	0 - 3
330	6	4 – 5	7 – 8	4 - 5
350	7	6	9 – 10	6
370	8	7	11 – 12	7
400	9 – 10	8	13 – 14	8
430	11 -12	9	15 – 16	9
450	13 – 14	10	17 – 18	10
470	15	11	19 – 20	11
500	16	12	21 – 22	12
530	17 – 18	13	23 – 24	13
550	19 -20	14 – 15	25 – 26	14 - 15
570	21 – 22	16 -17	27 – 29	16
600	23 – 24	18 -19	30 – 32	17
630	25 – 26	20 – 21	33 – 34	18

650	27 – 28	22 – 23	35 – 36	19
670	29 – 30	24	37	20
700	31	25	38 – 39	21
730	32	26	40 – 41	22
750	33	27	42 – 43	23
770	34	28	44 – 45	24
800	35 – 36	29	46 – 47	25
830	37 – 38	30	48 – 49	26
850	39 – 40	31 – 32	50 – 51	27
890	41 – 42	33 – 34	52 – 53	28
900	43 – 44	35 – 36	54 – 55	29

Fill-in Worksheets

Set: Fill-in Worksheet

Assessment Type: Whether the respective university uses the 'ranking' or 'cut-off' method to assess the UKCAT.

Application:Place Ratio: The ratio of how many students apply versus the number of places on the course. (Refer to Step 1: Set)

UKCAT Score: The minimum UKCAT required for the respective university (based on research findings)

University	Assessment Type	Application: Places Ratio	UKCAT Score

Ideal Target Practice Score: _____

Minim Target Practice Score: _____

Identify: Fill-in Worksheet

Official Practice Test Results

	Practice Test A	Practice Test B	Practice Test C	Average Score
Verbal Reasoning (out of 44)				
Decision Making (out of 29)				
Quantitative Reasoning (out of 36)				
Abstract Reasoning (out of 55)				

Official Practice Test Results (out of 900)

	Average Score (Out of 900)	Last Year UKCAT Statistics
Verbal Reasoning		
Quantitative Reasoning		
Abstract Reasoning		
Decision Making		

Prioritise: Fill-in Worksheet

	Average Practice Score (out of 900)	Last Year Averages (out of 900)	Percentage difference
Verbal Reasoning			
Quantitative Reasoning			
Abstract Reasoning			
Decision Analysis			

Priority Table

Amount of Practice Test: This refers to the minimum amount of time you intend to spend preparing for each subtest (Refer to Step 3: Prioritise).

Priority	Subtest	Amount of Practice Time
1st		
2nd		
3rd		
4th		

Improve: Fill-in Worksheet

List the top THREE tips, tactics or techniques that works well for you in each subtest

Verbal Reasoning

    1. _____

    2. _____

    3. _____

Quantitative Reasoning

    1. _____

    2. _____

    3. _____

Abstract Reasoning

    1. _____

    2. _____

    3. _____

Decision Making

    1. _____

    2. _____

    3. _____

Situational Judgement

    1. _____

    2. _____

    3. _____

Assess: Fill-in Worksheet

Error Rate

Subtests	Error Rate (%)		
	Mock 1	Mock 2	Mock 3
Verbal Reasoning			
Quantitative Reasoning			
Abstract Reasoning			
Decision Making			
Situational Judgement			

Mock Test Results Analysis

	vs Average	vs Target	vs Previous Mock	Weakest Subtest
Mock Test 1			N/A	
Mock Test 2				
Mock Test 3				

32943969R00123

Printed in Great Britain
by Amazon